Raymond Lamont-Brown

Chambers

CHAMBERS
An imprint of Larousse plc
43–45 Annandale Street
Edinburgh EH7 4AZ

First published by Chambers 1994

A CIP catalogue record for this book is available from the British Library

ISBN 0 550 20075 4

Illustrations by John Marshall

Typeset by Pillans & Wilson Ltd
Edinburgh, Glasgow, London and Manchester
Printed in Singapore by
Singapore National Printers Ltd

Contents

Introduction: The Witches Forgather 1

Whence Came Scotland's Witches? 6

The Great Witch Trials 16

The Devil and All His Works 42

Sabbats and Feasts 54

The Scottish Witches' Gardens 68

Black Cats and Horned Toads 79

Cures, Curses and Charms 93

A Witch Gazetteer 107

Introduction: The Witches Forgather

'We naturally expect that the Scotch (as it was still possible to describe my sensitive kinsmen)—a people renowned from the earliest times for their powers of imagination—should be more deeply imbued with this gloomy supersitition [witchcraft] than their neighbours of the south. The nature of their soil and climate tended to encourage the dreams of early ignorance. Ghosts, goblins, wraiths, kelpies and a whole host of spiritual beings, were familiar to the dwellers by the misty glens of the Highlands, and the romantic streams of the Lowlands.'
Memoirs of Extraordinary Popular Delusions (1841) Charles Mackay

It lies on a grassy knoll in a field flanking the B8062 from Dunning to Auchterarder in Perthshire. At first sight the cairn surmounted by a cross looks like a war memorial. Alas it has a more sinister history; a close look at the rough, misshapen painted lettering reveals that the hand-hewn pile of stones is in fact a monument to one 'Maggie Walls, burned here 1657 as a witch'.

Probably the only commemorative cairn to a witch in the whole of Europe, the cross is nonetheless mysterious, for there is no record of a Maggie Walls in the major Scottish trial records and none of the locals can explain the origins of the memorial. Although the cross is rude and by no means the work of craftsmen, it is a reminder of the lengths to which men went to purge their home areas of witchcraft. In 1663 James, Lord Ruthven with several other local Dunning gentry condemned to death no less than 11 witches; some were put to death by drowning in the River

Earn, others by strangulation and burning at Kincladie Wood.

The witchcraft of common folklore is a medieval concept, and it is one of the greatest and most widespread confidence tricks ever perpetrated on society. Indeed its belief was universal in Britain, and every county has its individual witchlore. And the belief lingered long in Scotland.

As late as 1883 the Sheriff Court at Inverness heard a case in which a *carp creagh* (clay image) was presented in evidence in a dispute between two quarrelling women. The four-inch image, wound with green thread and pierced with pins, had been used by one woman in an attempt to work sympathetic magic (a mimed ritual to bring about an evil result) against the other.

Similarly, a 'cursing bone' was discovered in the house of a locally reputed witch in Glen Shira, Argyll, at her death, by the local minister, the Rev J Findley Dawson. He gave it to a retired teacher, Miss Helen Warwick, who presented it to the Scottish National Museum of Antiquities in 1944. The 'bone' consisted of a length of deer bone which pierced a thick oval ring of bog oak. Such artefacts were long used in the Highlands to fix a curse on anyone who had crossed a supposed witch.

During October 1947 a last testament was

contested in the Scottish Land Court at Stornoway, on the premise that the testator had believed in witchcraft. He had accused his neighbour of walking in a circle three times widdershins (against the sun) to put a spell on his livestock, as a result of which some of them had gone lame. In giving his ruling the judge, Lord Gibson, noted: 'Even supposing it had been proved that he was superstitious, there is not a tittle of evidence that any belief he had held had affected his ability to make a will'.

Belief in witchcraft in Scotland developed into a superstitious ideology shared by Scotland's royal house, bishops and peasants alike. Even members of the aristocracy were deemed dabblers, it will be seen, like Sir Robert Gordon of Gordonstoun, bynamed 'The Warlock', who was a man of science and a courtier of James II. Gordon and other Scots gentry studied the 'Black Arts' at the schools of magic at Padua, Italy and Salamanca, Spain. Witch hunts, then, were invariably led by educated men, although many accusations came from the illiterate.

Scotland's evolved beliefs in witchcraft went hand in hand with fairy lore to give the superstition surrounding witchcraft an origin in nature. This was picked up by Scots witch hunters to prove that witchcraft skills could be inherited and that witchcraft had a history of its own. On 28 May 1588, for instance, at the trial of Alison Piersoun at Byrehill, Fife, her indictment was for 'hanting and repairing with guid nichbouris [the fairies] and Quene of Elfhame thir divers zeiris [years] bypast'. And she confessed that 'in Grangenuir thair come ane man to hir cled in grene cloathis, quha said to hir, gif [if] scho wald be faithful he would do her gude.' The inference was clear to any witch hunter that the man was dressed as a wizard and induced her to join his group to work nature magic.

Despite the fact that Scotland has one of the most comprehensive collections of witch trial documentation in Europe covering the period 1500–1727, it was not until the Victorian age that local historians took time to actually define the

Scottish witch as she appeared in Scottish parlance. Writing in 1881 from his manse at Pitsligo, Aberdeen, the Rev Walter Gregor composed a classic example:

'The witch was usually an old woman, who lived in a lonely house by herself, and kept all her affairs very much to herself. Her power was derived from Satan, and was very great, and ranged over almost everything. By various ways she could cause disease in man and beast; raise storms to destroy crops, sink ships, and do other destructive work; steal cows' milk, and keep herself well supplied with milk and butter, though she had no cow. To do this last she was able to turn herself into a hare. At times, however, she used her power for the benefit of those who pleased her. She could cure diseases, discover stolen goods, and tell who a thief was. Such a woman was dreaded . . . The power of witchcraft was sometimes possessed by men. It was also inherent in certain families, and went down from generation to generation'.

Such witchcraft historians as Rossell Hope Robbins and Pennethorne Hughes underlined the fact that Scotland was second only to Germany in 'the barbarity' of its witch persecution and trials. As Robbins says: 'The Presbyterian clergy acted like inquisitors, and the church sessions often shared the prosecution with the secular law courts.'

Robbins goes on: 'The Scottish laws were, if anything, more heavily loaded against the accused. Finally, the devilishness of the torture was limited only by Scotland's backward technology in the construction of mechanical devices. Suppression of any opposition to belief in witchcraft was complete.

'To the end of the sixteenth century, while there is evidence of considerable magic and sorcery of a simple folklore nature . . . trials for witchcraft were few. Up to the Reformation, there was not one case of *burning for witchcraft*'.

The extant documents on witch history in Scotland certainly bear out these comments. Why should it be so? Why did John Knox and the Regent

Moray, for instance, pursue what the country's medieval clergy had largely ignored? The answer lies in the reformed clergy's adherence to a belief in the literal truth of the Gospels. So such authority as Exodus 22:18, 'Thou shalt not suffer a witch to live', was inherent in the Common Law of Scotland. Thus from 1560 or so Scottish witch trials were to develop overtones of religious animosity and political struggle.

Following the repeal of the laws against witchcraft, interest in the subject diminished. However, Victorian and Edwardian local historians did include mentions of local witchcraft delusion in their histories, and from the 1920s folklorists began to recognise the importance of the occurrences of witchlore belief in the fabric of the folklore and history of Scotland.

Whence Came Scotland's Witches?

His picture made in wax, and gently molten
By a blue fire, kindled with dead men's eyes
Will waste him by degrees.
The Witch Thomas Middleton (1570–1627)

When the Roman Soldiers disappeared into the mists of the Cheviot Hills for the last time, they left behind them the seeds of Christianity. Here and there were pockets of this new religion living alongside a thousand-year-old pagan belief of dark happenings, demons and shaman-soothsayers. On this scant Christian base, though, the celebrated missionaries such as Ninian, Columba, Kentigern (bynamed Mungo) and Cuthbert organized their churches.

Decades later the medieval chroniclers were to use the traditional belief in witchcraft to underline the miraculous nature of the work of these missionaries. For example, in the 11th century a chronicler noted how St Patrick, patron saint of Ireland, was born at Dumbarton. Patrick's piety, says the chronicler, was feared by the Devil himself, who in 388 incited 'the whole body of witches in Scotland against him'. Patrick fled down the Clyde in a small boat and made for Ireland. As everyone knows, affirms the chronicler, witches cannot cross running water, so they plucked a huge rock and threw it at the unfortunate Patrick. They missed, but in time the rock became famous as the fortress of Dumbarton.

The old gods of the early inhabitants of Scotland were to become the adversaries of the Christian God and his missionaries like Patrick; and memories of the pagan deities were focused into the persona of what the medieval clerics saw as the Devil. All things not understood by the populace, or that were contrary to Christianity, became

witchcraft, and as every leader must have followers those who were not devotees of the Christian God must be Devil-worshipping witches.

From the beginning of tribal life in Scotland there were always men and women who were deemed to have a secret knowledge of the workings of Nature and the fashioning of charms and cures. As the early tribesmen of Scotland needed adequate food supplies, shelter and clothing, it was the task of these knowledgeable ones to perform rites by which the necessities might be secured. Among the ancient gospels of the supernatural arts there was the cult of feminism, and from the mid-ninth millennium BC Europe saw the evolution of the matriarchal cult in which caves, woodlands and stars were all revered as female emblems. Soon those selected to petition the gods for benefices would be exclusively female; for women, with their own fertile powers to reproduce life, were deemed the closest beings to Mother Nature.

It is easy to deduce how white (good) magic could be reversed into black (evil) magic by the fearful, and the comely maidens who danced in the sacred groves be aped by the 'wither'd beldams' and 'rigwoodie hags' described by Robert Burns (1759–96) in *Tam o'Shanter*. As the European poet Volle wrote:

When Satan, for weighty dispatches,
Sought messengers cunning and bold,
He passed by the beautiful faces,
And pick'd out the ugly and old.

By about AD750, the areas we know as Scotland today, then inhabited by Scots, Picts, Britons and English, supported and followed a Christian clergy. As these early Christian clergymen went about their business, they paid little heed to the pagan superstitions around them, and up to the year 1200 or so cases of so-called witchcraft in Scotland are seldom recorded. When purported sorcerers were put to death they were not indicted for witchcraft as such but for committing, or attempting to commit, murder. Witness the case of the witches mentioned by the historian George Buchanan (1506–82) in his *History of Scotland:* Buchanan tells how King Duffus (962–6), son of Malcolm I, was attacked by a group of three witches who 'roasted' a wax image of Duffus 'upon a wooden spit, reciting certain words of enchantment, and basting the figure with a poisonous liquor'. When apprehended, the triad of women admitted attempting to harm Duffus by enchantment. They were burned at Cluny Hill, Forres, in Moray for their pains; today they are remembered by the local 'Witches Stone' and as one of the first recorded witch executions in Scotland.

Two types of witch evolved from the old Scots lore. The story of Duffus reveals type one—the hag-witch of superstition accredited with evil occult powers. The Weird Sisters of MacBeth's legends however were Scottish witches of the other type, 'those supernatural beings who interfered with the affairs of this world, but were not of it' (Clark *Shakespeare and the Supernatural* p26).

MacBeth, son of Doada (daughter of Malcolm II) and Findlaech MacRuaridh, Mormaer of Moray, was born in 1005. Shakespeare drew the Weird Sisters for his play *Macbeth* (1606) from hints in the *Chronicles* of Ralph Holinshed (d1580), a dash of Scottish folklore gossip from the court of James VI and I, and a goodly dose of comment from the

Latin History of Scotland by Hector Boece (c1465–1536). It was Boece who identified the Weird Sisters and inspired Shakespeare to create the half-earthly, half-metaphysical beings of his play who had the power to raise spirits.

By the 11th century scholars such as Burchard of Worms, in his *Patrologia Latina*, were denouncing a belief in witchcraft as 'a heinous sin', and in 1180 John of Salisbury, Bishop of Chatres—advisor to Thomas Becket, Archbishop of Canterbury, patron of the monks of Arbroath Abbey—was gathering notes on what witchcraft belief might be. Salisbury mentions how witches were talked of as assembling for feasts and stealing children, yet he dismisses all the findings as illusions of a fevered imagination. Around the 12th century too, Scottish scholars were hearing stories of how people were making compacts with the fallen angel, the Devil. Slowly a case for belief in witchcraft was being built.

By the 13th century, the Congregation of the Holy Inquisition—the medieval Church's watchdog on heterodoxy against the faith—was successfully including within its jurisdiction sorcery, now proclaimed a heresy. This was well established in the statutes of the Cistercian order by 1290 for instance as the sin of heresy brought about by magic practices, and the Cistercians had an influential dozen or so houses in Scotland. For the first time in Scotland, influenced by European thought, witchcraft was inextricably mixed with the politics of the church.

In the reign of William I, the Lion (1143–1214), there began to emerge certain personalities whose prophecies and purported magical activities brought them within the medieval definition of witch-sorcerer. Thus witches and wizards began to slip in and out of Scottish literature and history with an ease which added to their credibility.

Head and shoulders above them all was Sir Michael Scott (c1160–1238) of Balweary, near Kirkcaldy, Fife. Chroniclers say that Scott studied Arabic, astronomy and chemistry at Oxford, mathematics and theology at Paris, and his occult skills at the famous School of Magic at Padua, Italy. His magic dexterity was even mentioned by the Italian poet Dante (1265–1321) in his *Inferno:*

> . . . Michael Scott,
> Practised in every slight of magic wile.

Michael Scott's career remains hazy, but his fame was given a boost in Scotland's witchcraft history as 'a wizard' in Sir Walter Scott's (1771–1832) *The Lay of the Last Minstrel* (1805):

> In these far climes it was my lot
> To meet the wondrous Michael Scott;
> A wizard of such dreadful fame . . .

This encouraged Fife poet William Tennant (1784–1848) to mention the wizard in his *Anster Fair* (1812):

> With her resided that fam'd wizard old,
> Her uncle and her guardian, Michael Scot,
> Who there, in Satan's arts malignly bold,
> His book of dev'lish efficacy wrote . . .
> And, lackey'd round (tremendous to be told!)
> With demons hung with tails like shaggy goat,
> Employ'd their ministrations damn'd to ring
> . . .

According to the tradition recounted by W Henderson in the 'Witch of Falsehope', Michael Scott was turned 'into a hare' and was hunted by his own hounds (see page 111). Again tradition has Michael Scott at the Cistercian Abbey of Glenluce, Wigtownshire, where he taught local witches to plait sand. This natural phenomenon of sand in rope-like patterns can still be seen in Luce Bay. Walter Scott has his namesake buried at Melrose Abbey in the south presbytery chapel of St Martin. Here Scott pointed out a boss in the likeness of the wizard, and added that he had given the nearby Eildon Hills their distinctive shape by cleaving them in two by magic.

Its damp walls, dark shadows and green-slimed storage undercrofts make Hermitage Castle, Roxburghshire, an eerie ruin in which to recall one of the most hated and feared of its former owners. Sited in Liddesdale, the castle is most remembered today as the trysting place of Mary, Queen of Scots, who visited her wounded lover James Hepburn, Earl of Bothwell, in 1566. And even then they talked of the phantom footfalls of the 'witchmaster' William de Soulis, lord of Liddesdale, who held the castle in the days of Robert I, the Bruce (1274–1329) and who was the Hereditary Butler of Scotland.

De Soulis was to become the quintessential evil Scottish landowner who abused his position through witchcraft for generations of Scottish writers. De Soulis was said to conduct 'foul sorceries' and 'every species of wickedness' in his castle. Local traditions made him a pupil of Michael Scott and identified him as the murderer of Kieldar Mangerton, bynamed Cout of Keilder, in Cout's Pool in the Scottish Border hills. This drowning was the last straw for the locals of Liddesdale who petitioned King Robert to have the 'witchmaster' executed. 'Hang him, boil him, do what you like with him,' Robert is reported to have said, 'but let me hear no more of him'.

Sir Walter Scott in his *Border Minstrelsy* tells how de Soulis was boiled to death in a cauldron of molten lead up on Nine Stane Rig by his neighbours. In truth though, William de Soulis, one of the signatories of the Declaration of Arbroath, was indicted for treason in 1320 and condemned to perpetual imprisonment at Dumbarton Castle. Yet so feared was he in Liddesdale for his supposed witchcraft that the locals and their descendants preferred the tale of boiling to death over historical truth. Thus was the gentle curative nature magic of Scotland's tribal shamans given a sinister overtone in medieval times by projecting it into the realm of witchcraft. The same was to be done to the clergy who attracted public odium.

The *Chronicon de Lanercost* tells us that in 1282 Father John, parish priest of Inverkeithing, induced young village girls to caper in a dance in 'honour of Father Liber' (Liber was an ancient Italian priapic diety). Then, heading the girls in a lewd troop, Father John danced ahead 'carrying on a pole a representation of the human organ of generation', stirring them all 'to lust and filthy language'.

So by the 13th century sexuality and blasphemy were being mixed with supposed witchcraft practices. What was more significant, too, was that heresy, brought about by magic practices, began to emerge as a political tool.

The Eildon Hills, which according to Walter Scott had been cleft by his namesake, were also linked with Sir Thomas Learmonth of Ercildoun Tower (c1200–97), known as Thomas the Rhymer, who has a page or two of his own in Scotland's history of witchcraft. A landowner in the area we know as Earlston, Berwickshire, Learmonth was probably the illegitimate issue of one of the Cospatrick earls of Dunbar. Legend says that Thomas was the captive of the Queen of Elfland and for seven years was her prisoner by enchantment under the Eildon Hills. There he was given the gift of prophecy. Thomas is quoted as having predicted the succession of Robert I, the Bruce on the death of Alexander III in 1286 and to have prophesied the Union of the Crowns in this couplet:

> When Tweed and Powsail meet at Merlin's Grave
> England and Scotland shall one monarch have.

(Merlin's Grave is sited at Drumelzier, southwest of Peebles, and local legend has it that on the day of James VI's accession the Tweed overflowed into the Powsail Burn.)

It must be said that Thomas's prophecies did not appear in literary form until the 15th century, thus making them dubious in origin, but it is interesting to note how in this century prophecy was being linked to witchcraft.

Great architectural works were also cited as being made possible through witchcraft. A contemporary of Thomas Learmonth is referred to in this connection: Hugh Gifford of Yester, averred the chronicler-chantry priest of Aberdeen John of Fordun (c1320–84), did 'by magic art' construct for himself a 'cavern' called Bohall ('Hobgobin Hall') at Yester Castle, near Gifford, East Lothian.

John Pinkerton (1758–1826), the Edinburgh-born historian and antiquary, printed a contemporary account of the assassination of James I at Perth on 21 February 1437. The account shows how popular witchlore was traditionally threaded into the stories of royal murder by violence.

The report recounted how James, *en route* from Edinburgh to Perth, was about to cross the Water of Leith when a witch appeared at the side of the road and prophesied his death: 'My lord king, as ye pass this water, ye shall never turne again and live'. In some perplexity, though mollified somewhat by his attendant declaring 'she is but a drunken fool', James rode on. Again the witch, described as being Irish, mysteriously entered the king's court circle at Perth and petitioned the king to allow her to speak with him some more about her prophecy. James told her to return on the morrow—the day he was assassinated by Sir Robert Stewart and Sir Robert Graham at Perth's Dominican Friary.

Another story of witchcraft and murder associated with royalty was set down by George Buchanan in his *History of Scotland*. Rumours abounded—mostly from the tongue of the royal favourite Thomas Cochrane—of how Prince John Stewart, Earl of Mar, directed magical practices against his brother James III (1452–88). It seems to have been common knowledge that Mar was much celebrated for the study of witchcraft and he met his end, according to Buchanan, for practising the Black Arts.

Around the same time as Mar's indictment, a dozen women as well as a handful of men were arrested, charged with employing witchcraft against the king in aid of Mar. They were all executed by fire at Craig Gate (Calton Hill) Edinburgh and Mar, an erstwhile prisoner at Craigmillar Castle, bled to death in Edinburgh's Canongate in 1479 in suspicious circumstances.

The great watershed of witch persecution in Europe by the medieval Church followed the publication of the book *Malleus Maleficarum,* 'Hammer of the Witches', in 1486. By the end of the 15th century the belief that witchcraft was a dangerous reality had received a strong impetus through the promulgation of the Bull of Pope Innocent VIII, called *Summis desiderentes affectibus,* of 9 December 1484. In it he expressed distress that in parts of Christendom there were those who embarked upon 'carnal alliances with devils' and 'by their incantations, charms, and other abominable superstitions and sortileges' were bewitching humans and animals.

The enforcement of this bull was placed in the hands of two fanatical Dominican priests, Jacob Sprenger, Prior of the Convent of Cologne (1436–95), and Prior Inquisitor Heinrich Kramer (c1490–1505), who put together the book *Malleus Maleficarum.* It was a total fabrication of supposed witch practices, fables and myths, and became the 'textbook for judges or secular courts' charged with the prosecution of witch trials.

From this point evangelical Catholics and Protestants in equal measure rivalled each other in the zeal of their persecution of witchcraft. And the *Malleus Maleficarum* became the text of sermons for figures such as Martin Luther (1483–1546, himself a renegade Dominican), who influenced Scotland's Reformation, and John Knox (1505–72), Scotland's most famous reformer, who expertly juxtaposed 'the Devil, the Mass and Witches' for his own denominational ends.

Thus Catholic and Protestant writers alike drew on each other for proof of witchcraft. By the 16th century, the beginning of the great witch trials of Scotland, witchcraft had evolved from the early practices of fertility magic in the tribal lands in the sequence opposite:

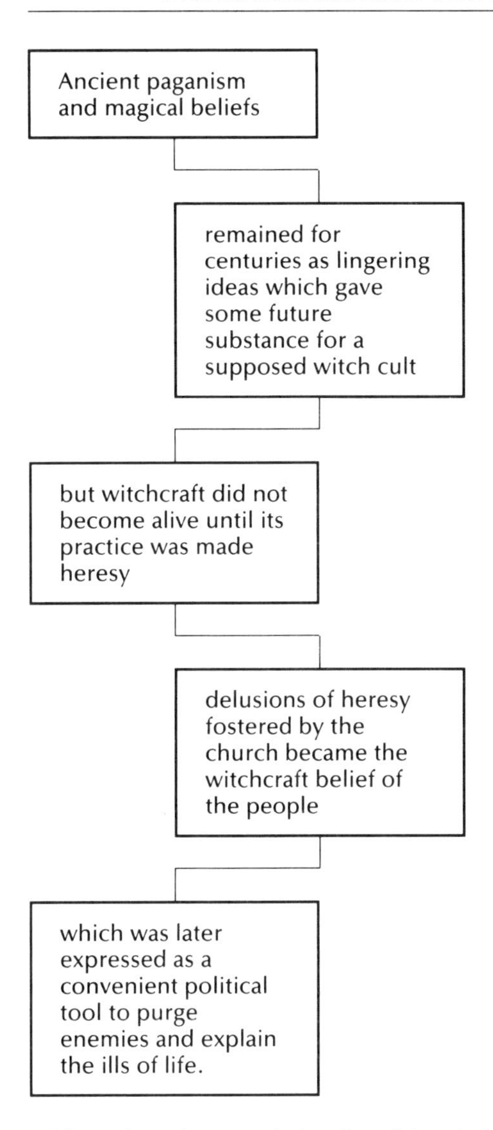

Thus the picture of the Scottish witch was evolved—and he or she was deemed to dwell in the midst of any community rich or poor.

The Great Witch Trials

The foul thief knotted the tether,
She lifted his head on hie,
The nourice drew the knot
That gar'd Laird Warriston die.
Ballads James Jamieson (1759–1838)

During June 1563 the Scottish Parliament passed a statute against witchcraft as the Seventy-Third Act of the Ninth Parliament of Queen Mary recorded under *Acta Parliamentorum Mariae*. In truth it only served to help confirm all the established superstitious prejudices against witchcraft, for within its wording the statute did not recognize a crime of witchcraft. Instead it referred to the pretence of being a witch, and blasphemy by purporting to use 'Sorcerie'.

A short while after the Act, two witches were burned in the 'Northland' on the cognizance of the queen's bastard brother James Stewart, Earl of Moray (1531–70). In Fife and Galloway a few supposed witches were warned by the courts for practising witchcraft; in Dunfermline Agnes Mullikine, an alias of Bessie Boswell, was 'banist and exilt for witchcraft'.

From the supposed enchantment of James III to the passing of the 1563 Act there were few witch cases noted. In St Andrews in 1542 the *Rentale Sancti Andree* notes that three witches were burned at Witches' Hill at a cost of £3.18s (£3.90), but this was exceptional. Nevertheless, in 1537 a witch execution had set Scotland ablaze with horrified gossip.

It was the story of Janet, Lady Douglas, sister of the Earl of Angus, widow of John Lyon, Lord Glamis. Along with her second husband Archibald Campbell of Kepneith, her son and an elderly priest, Janet was accused of plotting the death by poison and evil charms of James V (1512–42). She was found guilty and consigned to the flames on Castlehill, Edinburgh. Janet was a victim not of witchcraft but of the politics of the time and James V's pathological suspicousness.

Up to 1590 or so only a few other witch cases received more than a passing mention in Scottish historical record. The murder of Mary, Queen of Scots's repellent husband Henry Stewart, Lord Darnley, in 1567 did give rise to one witch accusation of note: George Buchanan commented in his *Detection* that Janet, Lady Scott of Buccleuch (d1568) was generally credited with having 'gained the queen's consent to the murder of Darnley through her witchcraft'. No evidence was ever brought against Lady Buccleuch.

Richard Bannatyne (d1605), secretary to John Knox, noted in his *Journal* for 3 July 1571 how Margaret Stewart, Countess of Athole, was 'much accused' for practising the 'black art'. Bannatyne repeated the gossip that 'at the birth of James VI, [the countess] cast the pains of childbirth from [Mary, Queen of Scots] on to [Margaret Forbes] Lady Rires' by incantation. As in the case of Lady Buccleuch, no evidence was brought against Lady Athole.

As the use of witchcraft as a political tool grew in popularity—for an accusation of witchcraft was deemed unanswerable—certain families which fell out of favour with the ruling cadre were subtly branded as witchkeepers. In this way their influence and credibility could be undermined. The Ker family were one such target.

In the curious document *Staggering State of Scots Statesmen* is found this accusation against the family of Mark Ker, Commendator (1587) of the former Cistercian Abbey of Newbattle and prominent courtier as Master of Requests to James VI:

'He had by his wife, the Lord Herries's daughter, thirty-one children. His lady always kept in her company . . . witches, and especially one Margaret Nues (Innes), who fostered his daughter, the Lady Borthwick, who was long after his death burnt in Edinburgh for that crime; and my Lady Lothian's son-in-law, Sir Alexander Hamilton, told one of his friends, how one night lying in Prestongrange, pertaining to the said abbey of Newbattle, he was pulled out of his bed by the said witches, and sore beaten; of which injury, when he complained to his mother-in-law, and assured her he would complain thereof to the Council, she pacified him by giving him a purse full of gold. That lady thereafter, being vexed with a cancer in her breast, implored the help of a notable warlock, by a by-name called Playfair, who condescended to heal her, but with condition, that the sore should fall on them that she loved best; whereunto she agreeing did convalesce; but the Earl, her husband, found the boil in his throat, of which he died shortly thereafter; and the said Playfair being soon apprehended, was made a prisoner at Dalkeith steeple, and having confest that and much more wickedness to Mr Archibald Simpson, minister there, and that confession coming to the ears of Robert, Earl of Lothian . . . he had moyen to get some persons admitted to speak with the prisoner in the night, by which means he was found worried in the morning, and the point of his breeches knit about his neck, but never more enquiry was made who had done the deed'.

During the first decade or so of the Reformation the superstition linking witchcraft with the age-old Scottish belief in Elfame (fairyland) was promoted in Scottish witch accusations. The papers of John Knox's secretary Bannatyne give proof of this. The year was 1572 and Knox had spoken from the pulpit accusing a witch nicknamed Nicniven (a soubriquet for the Queen of Elfame), who was later condemned to death. Further, in 1576 Bessie Dunlop of Lyne, Ayrshire was burned, accused of belonging to 'a conclave of witches' and of receiving herbal cures from the Queen of Elfame. In 1588 Alison Piersoun of Byrehill, Fife, was convicted of 'practising sorcery, and invoking the foul fiend'. She too admitted to being 'intimate with the Queen of Elfame', which sealed her execution.

There were to be three major eras of witch

persecution in Scotland, 1590–97, 1640–44 and 1660–63, each throwing up witch trials which were classics in the history of Scottish witchcraft. The worst periods of persecution coincided with the dominance of fanatical Presbyterianism. In both 1640 and 1642, for example, the General Assembly of the Kirk promoted vigilance amongst ministers to search out witches and punish them.

Writing in *Rowan Tree and Red Thread* (1949), Thomas Davidson observes that when the medieval Church was swept away 'one ecclesiastical tyranny was replaced by another infinitely more oppressive'. Davidson continues:

'Under the Reformed faith, the infallibility of the Church was replaced by the infallibility of the Bible, and the worship of the Bible as the indisputable word of God completely changed the outlook of an entire nation. In Scotland the character of theology was even more severe than in other Puritan countries because the Scottish Kirk was unquestionably the result of a democratic movement, and her ministers arrogated to themselves a kind of infallibility in all matters of a political nature, with the result that Scotland became absolutely subservient to her clergy. The continued acceptance of superstition accommodated under a new name, as was the case in the Roman faith [ie, the medieval Church], was considered treason to God and so the Kirk, taking the Devil in its stride as a ready-made object lesson, proceeded to stamp him out.'

The scholar H T Buckle in his *History of Civilisation in England* (1925), shows how cleverly Scotland's ministers were empowered to deal with witch accusations:

'According to the Presbyterian policy, which reached its height in the 17th century, the clergyman of the parish selected a certain number of laymen on whom he could depend, and who, under the name of elders, were his councillors, or rather the ministers of his authority. They, when assembled together, formed what was called the Kirk Session, and this little court, which enforced the decisions uttered in the pulpit, was so supported by the superstitious reverence of the people that it was more powerful than any civil tribunal . . . Against such weapons, in such a state of society, resistance was impossible. The clergy interfered with every man's private concerns, ordered how he should govern his family, and often took upon themselves the personal control of his household. Their minions, the elders, were everywhere, for each parish was divided into several quarters, and to each quarter one of these officials was allotted in order that he might take special notice of what was done in his district. Besides this, spies were appointed so that nothing could escape their supervision. Not only streets but even private houses were searched and ransacked to see if anyone was absent from church while the minister was preaching. To him all must listen and all must obey. Without the consent of his tribunal no person might engage himself either as a domestic servant or as a field labourer.'

So the net against witchcraft and superstitious rituals was tight. And as an extra safety factor the 'spies' against witchcraft were given official authority. This is confirmed by G Dalyell in *Darker Superstitions of Scotland* (1834). The book cites, under 1603, the College of Aberdeen in Solemn Synod charging every minister to undertake a 'subtle and privy inquisition' in his parish to question all parishioners, upon oath, as to their knowledge of witchcraft practice and witches. And to make the decanting of 'knowledge' easier, kists (chests) were placed in all the churches so that the spies could drop in their written accusations.

From the records of witchcraft in Scotland, 10 cases emerge as major trials, each illuminating facets of the law and types of delusion. One of the most famous was this:

John Fian and the North Berwick Witches, 1590–2

This trial had a direct influence in hardening the witchcraft superstitions of James VI. It was an important case in the history of Scottish witchcraft for its use of torture, the description of covens and supposed rituals therein and its indictment of prominent citizens. No less significant was its use as a political tool against the Earl of Bothwell. In all, 70 people were implicated on charges of witchcraft and treason, but the exact number of executions is not known.

The foundation of this trial at Edinburgh and Prestonpans began with the suspicions of David Seaton, Deputy-bailiff of Tranent, concerning a young servant girl Gilly Duncan. She had the gift of healing people with herbal concoctions and what would pass today as faith healing, and was so skilled that Seaton deemed her facility 'unnatural and devilish'. He arrested Gilly and pronounced a mole on her neck to be the 'devil's mark', and under torture she 'confessed' to Seaton 'the wicked allurements and enticements of the devil'. In due time Gilly was coerced to name her 'accomplices' in what Seaton and his supporters believed to be witchcraft. She named several people including the well-educated and respected Agnes Sampson of Nether Keith, Barbara Napier, sister-in-law of the Laird of Carschoggill and Dr John Fian.

Because of her prominent role in society Agnes Sampson intrigued the king and he interviewed her at Holyrood Palace. James was a firm believer in witchcraft and he was to write an account of his superstition in *Daemonologie* (1597) as a consequence of the subsequent trial. Under cruel torture Agnes Sampson eventually confessed to

using charms for cures and attending covens to call up and honour the Devil at North Berwick churchyard. What most horrified the king was the acknowledgement that she and others had sailed the Forth in magic sieves and had plotted how to assassinate James as he voyaged to Norway to collect his new bride, Anne of Denmark, who he had married in 1589.

As time passed Agnes Sampson's confessions became more incredible, to include carromancy (the use of wax images), theriomancy (magic with animals) and necromancy (calling up the dead). Her indictment was backed by the king and she was executed at Haddington.

Another accomplice Dame Euphemia Maclean, daughter of the law senator Thomas Maclean, Lord Cliftonhall, was also found guilty and executed on 25 July 1591. But Barbara Napier fared a little better. Although accused and dragged to the stake for burning like the others, she was reprieved on account of being pregnant.

Amongst the other prominent accused, Dr John Fian, also known as John Cunningham, a schoolmaster of Saltpans (Prestonpans), fared the worst. Fian was indicted as 'secretary' of the North Berwick Witch Coven, and therefore its ringleader. Fian was arraigned on 26 December 1590 on 20 charges including conspiracy with Satan to kill the king. He too confessed under duress but recanted, to confess again under hideous torture. King James insisted that he was guilty and Fian was burned at Castle Hill, Edinburgh, on 23 January 1591.

The trial threw up a number of interesting procedures in Scottish witch trials: the use of torture was not banned by Scottish law; a prisoner (if he could afford it) was permitted a lawyer; a confession was not necessary before conviction and execution; a general reputation of being a witch was deemed 'evidence'; and no appeal was acceptable after a dittay (indictment) had been drawn. Further, the trial was perhaps the best example in Scottish witchcraft history of grudges being expiated, with David Seaton and others venting their spleens on prominent people in their locality. And one other was to be tainted by the curse of North Berwick.

Despite his prominence at court, Francis Stewart, Fifth Earl of Bothwell (1563–1612), cousin of James VI and godson of Mary, Queen of Scots, became a thorn in the flesh of the king. In acts of supreme lunacy he made several attacks on royal residences in his opposition to some of James's policies. Using witchcraft as a political tool, the Privy Council accused him of witchcraft and treason; he stood trial on 10 August 1593. The prosecution tried to implicate him in the supposed witch regicides of North Berwick (many of whose more prominent members were known to be acquaintances of his). The prosecution was unsuccessful, yet some still pointed him out as the 'Devil of North Berwick', the man who had masterminded the witch covens.

The Aberdeen Witches, 1596

Witch persecution mania was stimulated at Aberdeen by the appearance of James VI's *Daemonologie*. As a result anyone concocting herbal cures and age-old natural remedies came under suspicion of witchcraft. The trials caused a wider interest to be taken in the supernatural, especially among the 'wilder' Scottish lairds. Costs set out for this trial are of particular interest. The trials resulted in the burning of 24 men and women.

Accusations in this case ranged from the bewitching of animals to the manufacture of charms to make men unfaithful to their wives. A typical Aberdeen 'witch' was Janet Wishart, who was indicted for casting a spell on Alexander Thomson giving him the ague. Likewise she was accused of bewitching Andrew Webster to death; others too were deemed driven to the grave by Wishart's evil glances. Her indictment showed accusations of raising storms, dismembering corpses and causing nightmares.

Some of the witches were tried by 'swimming'. They were bound doubled up, 'their two thumbs and their great toes together; for being thus cast in the water, they floated . . .' (and were thus deemed guilty; to drown was to be assumed innocent).

The cost of burning two witches at Aberdeen was £11 10s (£11.50) for 'peat, tar barrels and coals'. The execution of Janet Wishart and Isobel Crocher was just £5-8s-4d (£5.41), to include combustibles, the stake and a hangman's rope (for strangulation), and an executioner's fee of 13s 4d. (66½p).

The Isobel Grierson Case, 1607

This trial showed the first recorded break away from the old traditionally believed witch superstitions, although Scottish witches on the whole were much more imaginative than others in devising methods of tormenting their victims. Isobel Grierson's case was heard before the Supreme Criminal Tribunal and recorded in the books of Adjournal.

Isobel Grierson was the wife of a common labourer called John Bull from Prestonpans, East Lothian. She was indicted on six separate counts. The first related to a 'cruel hatred and malice' she had conceived against Adam Clark in 1605. The indictment read that Grierson 'in likeness of her own cat, accompanied with a great number of other cats, in a devilish manner, entered within their house, where they made a great and tearful noise and trouble; whereby the said Adam, then lying in bed with his wife, and servants that were then in the house, apprehended such a great fear that they were likely to go mad'. The Devil appeared also as 'a black man' and 'dragged the servant around the house by her hair, so that she was sick for six weeks'.

She was also accused of appearing as the Devil to torment William Burnet who 'pined away and died', and of casting sickness on Robert Peddan in 1598 for not paying her a debt of 9s 4d (46½p). He recovered after he paid the debt, but one day, he recounted, Isobel Grierson was passing the open window of his house when she stretched out her hand to stroke the cat lying in the window. At that

time Peddan was brewing ale which he said immediately turned sour in Grierson's presence; he told the court that the ale was 'altogether rotten and black, thick like gutter dirt, with a filthy and pestilent odour, that no man might drink nor feel [endure] the smell thereof'.

Grierson was also charged with 'conceiving a deadly intent' against Margaret Donaldson, the wife of Robert Peddan from 1600. She suspected that Grierson had made her ill and asked neighbours to intercede; Mrs Peddan recovered but Grierson was said to have thought that Margaret was 'defaming her as a witch' and cast another spell of illness on her with the injunction 'The faggot of Hell light on thee, and Hell's cauldron may thou seethe in'. Margaret took ill again.

The sixth indictment declared that Isobel Grierson was 'a common sorcerer and a witch, and abuser of the people, by laying in and taking off of sickness and diseases, and using all devilish and ungodly means to win her living; and [a] user of charms and other devilish practices'. The jury found Isobel Grierson guilty and she was strangled and burned on Castle Hill, Edinburgh, soon after her trial of 10 March 1607.

It is clear in this case that the personality of Isobel Grierson was such that she terrified people with her mere silent presence. That was enough for hysterical, impressionable people to fall ill at her every askew glance, for the power of suggestion in the superstitious gave credence to the potency of witchcraft.

The Trial of Margaret Barclay, 1618

This trial shows how deeply sunk in cruelty the inquisitors had become in 60 years of persecuting witches with vigour; even calling young children to testify against their parents. Sir Walter Scott was constrained by his reading of the case papers to write this in his *Letters on Demonology and Witchcraft* (1832): 'It is scarcely possible that, after reading such a story, a man of sense can listen for an instant to the evidence founded on confession thus obtained, which has been almost the sole reason by which a few individuals, even in modern times, have endeavoured to justify a belief in the existence of witchcraft'.

One Margaret Barclay, the wife of Archibald Dean, a burgess of Irvine, Ayrshire, had apparently been ill-used by her brother-in-law, John Deans, who had stolen from her, and her sister-in-law, Janet Lyal, who had slandered her. So aggrieved was she that she had raised an accusation of slander at the local Kirk Session, which, after due consideration, urged reconciliation. Disgruntled, Margaret Barclay agreed to offer the hand of friendship, but the injury still rankled.

About this time Provost Andrew Train of Irvine was about to send one of his ships abroad; a vessel which was to be skippered by John Dean. Margaret Barclay was heard by many to curse the ship with the sentiment that she hoped that it went to the bottom of the sea taking John Dean with it.

Some time later the ship became overdue at its home port and one itinerant named John Stewart, pretending to be clairvoyant, declared the vessel lost to Provost Train. This worked out to be a good guess as the vessel was later reported sunk near Padstow. Rather than being rewarded for his clairvoyance, John Stewart was implicated with

Margaret Barclay by the superstitious for the ship's demise; she for her 'imprecated curses' and he for his prior knowledge.

Stewart was arrested first, and proceeded to tell the authorities that Margaret Barclay had taught him magic practices and that he had watched her make 'clay figures' with two other women; one of these figures was to represent Provost Train and the other the ship that was soon to be stricken. For good measure Stewart added that the Devil had appeared in the form of 'a handsome black lap-dog'. All then went down to the sea and cast the figures into the waves 'after which', avowed Stewart, 'the sea raged, roared and became red like the juice of madder in a dyer's cauldron'.

One of the two other females identified by Stewart, Ishbel Insh, was next arrested and the authorities (including two local ministers) proceeded to extract from her eight-year-old daughter 'evidence' against her. In her fear Ishbel Insh attempted to escape from her prison (the belfry of Irvine kirk) and fell, dying a few days later.

Margaret Barclay and Stewart were now to be arraigned before the court and before their appearance were tortured at the instigation of the Earl of Eglington, a local magnate. Stewart somehow slipped his arm fetters in his cell and hanged himself with the ribbons of his bonnet. Under torture described by the noble earl as 'gentle',

Margaret Barclay made a confession containing all the usual devilish nonsense a mind in terror can manufacture. At her trial however she was clear-minded enough to say: 'All I have confessed was in agony of torture, and before God, all I have spoken is false and untrue'. The jury of her Irvine peers found her guilty and she was forthwith burned at the stake.

Alas, in her 'confession' Margaret Barclay implicated one Isobel Crawford, who was also arrested and tortured. She too died in the flames protesting her innocence to the last.

Perth Witch Trial, 1623

This case shows the great attraction which charms and cures had over orthodox medicine in the 17th century, and how belief in fairies even at this late date played a prominent part in Scottish witchcraft delusion.

Banishment (1580) for alleged witchcraft, public warnings (1581–2) of those suspected of witchcraft and executions in 1597 and 1612 were the only main mentions of witch activity in Perth before the trial of Isobel Haldane, 15–26 May 1623.

Haldane was convened before the Kirk Session of Perth accused of healing rituals in which sick children were washed and their sickbed clothes thrown in the River Tay. She was also accused of conversing with the fairy folk, endeavouring to lift from Patrick Ruthven, a weaver, the curse of bewitchment by another witch, and of herself cursing Stephen Ray of Muirton to death by a wasting disease.

Fragments of her interrogation by the Kirk Session exist and this is an example of their tone:
Question: *Where had she learned her skill?*
Answer: When I was lying in child bed lair, I was drawn forth from my bed to a dub [stagnant pool] near my house door in Dunning [a village in Perthshire], and was there puddled [confused] and troubled.
Question: *By whom was this done?*
Answer: By the fairy folks, who appeared some of them red, some of them gray, and riding upon

horses. The principal of them that spake to me was a bonny white man, riding upon a gray horse. He desired me to speak of God, and do good to poor folks; and he showed me the means how I might do this, which was by washing, bathing, speaking words, putting sick persons through hasps [skeins] of yarn, and the like.

The Glenluce Devil, 1654–6

This case was a clearly manufactured poltergeist manifestation which resulted in the death of an innocent beggar. Poltergeist is a term taken from the German for 'noisy spirit', but was not used in this connection in Britain until after 1848. Thus several Victorian writers referred to the case as the Glenluce Poltergeist.

The phoney psychic-troubles of the family of Gilbert Campbell, a weaver of Glenluce, near Newton Stewart, Galloway, were traced back by the superstitious to a *damnum minatum* (a curse) of Alexander Agnew, a beggar who had been refused a handout by the Campbells. This curse was utilized by a bright and conniving son of the house to further his own ends. Young Thomas Campbell was a brilliant scholar at the College (grammar school) at Glasgow. His father having fallen on hard times, Thomas feared that his education would be terminated, so in his twisted logic he resolved to punish his family for failing him by subjecting them to supposed evil spirits. This he would tie in with the old beggar's curse.

The family's torment began with strange whistling noises both inside and outside their home at Glenluce. On one occasion one of Thomas's sisters, Janet Campbell, was frightened on her way to the well by whistling taking the form of a disembodied voice saying 'I'll cast thee Janet into the well'.

A few months later, according to George Sinclair who recounted the story as a factual witch-tale in his *Satan's Invisible World Discovered* (1685), the 'Foul Fiend' (ie the Devil—in reality Thomas) began the traditional poltergeist activity of throwing stones at the house. These poltergeist manifestations also stripped the bedclothes off the sleeping Campbells and scattered clothes from trunks and chests.

At length Gilbert Campbell sent his children to neighbouring houses for safety and the activities stopped. When they returned, Thomas recommenced the torment including a few mysterious house fires put out before the house was engulfed.

The family now asked a local minister to come and pray for relief. There was a temporary reprieve but on 12 February 1654 the mysterious voice that Janet had heard began to echo through the house once more. So skilled was Thomas with his ventriloquism that many folk said the Campbells were actually able to converse with Satan; indeed the voice had learned discussions with the incredibly naive minister on theology and Latin texts.

Thomas kept up his mischief for almost two years and a Synod of Presbyters was set up to advise the Campbells. Eventually the beggar Agnew became implicated, even though he was not named by Thomas, who as the disembodied voice had listed local witches as the perpetrators of Satan's work at Glenluce. Agnew was executed at Dumfries for blasphemy and few later commentators doubted that Thomas's revenge against his father had caused the death.

Isobel Gowdie of Auldearn, 1662

This is perhaps the witch trial case that reveals most about Scottish witchcraft beliefs, and contains one of the clearest references to a coven and a sabbat. The claims made by Isobel Gowdie for Scottish witch practice were the popular beliefs of the period. The case also shows what deep inroads continental witch customs had made in Scottish witchcraft beliefs.

It appears that Isobel Gowdie, spouse of John Gilbert, gave her confessions without torture during four interrogations between 13 April and 27 May 1662. Today it seems clear that she was totally deranged, but she certainly believed what she said and her inquisitors carefully jotted down her claims of being able to turn herself into a jackdaw or a cat and of having learned how to fly through the air. Her favourite mode of transport was on straws blown in the wind, for which she summoned up the power by shouting, 'Horse and hattock in the Devil's name'.

Isobel Gowdie's career as a witch began in 1647, when she averred to have made a pact with the Devil at Auldearn Church in north-east Nairnshire. The ritual of the pact was described thus: she began by 'denying Christian baptism, receiving the new name of Janet, the Devil's mark on her shoulder, and rebaptism in her own blood which the Devil sucked from her. She swore allegiance by placing one hand on her head and the other on the sole of her foot. The ceremony concluded with the Devil . . . reading from the pulpit'.

The feast of the sabbat described by Isobel Gowdie began with a special witch grace:

We eat this meat in the Devil's name
With sorrow and sighs and mickle shame;
We shall destroy both house and hold;
Both sheep and cattle in the fold,
Little good shall come to the fore,
Of all the rest of the little store.

Isobel Gowdie also told her inquisitors that a true coven was made up of 13 witches (the number present at Christ's last supper) and each had a nickname like Swein, Rorie or the Roaring Lion.

Metamorphosis was a particular interest and skill of Isobel Gowdie, who liked to change herself into a cat with this personalized spell:

I shall go into a cat,
With sorrow and sigh and a little black shot.
And I shall go in the Devil's name
Ay while I come home again.

Isobel Gowdie was not the only witch to fall foul of the law at Auldearn in 1662. Katherine Sowter, the Witch of Bandon and Janet Breadheid were three others. And in the case of the latter witch at least a dozen more were named at her trial. The papers on all these trials held before Commissioner Sir Hew Campbell of Calder are incomplete, but it is likely that all the witches were executed.

Thomas Weir's Delusions, 1670

This case, another example of the accused being completely insane, is also indicative of the injustice of Scottish trial procedures in witchcraft cases even at this late date. Major Thomas Weir and his sister were brought to trial in Edinburgh on 6 April 1670.

Born around 1600, Weir is said to have come of good family in Lanarkshire and was one of the soldiers sent by the Scottish Covenanting Estates in 1641 to quell Irish Papists. He was Commander of the City Guard of Edinburgh in 1649, from which he obtained his military title. The Rev Frazer of Wardlaw described Weir thus in his *Divine Providences* (1670):

'His garb was still a cloak, and somewhat dark, and he never went without his staff. He was a tall black [ie swarthy] man, and ordinarily looked down to the ground; a grim countenance, and a big nose. At length he became so notoriously regarded among the Presbyterian strict sect, that if four met together, be sure Major Weir was one. At private meetings he prayed to admiration, which made many of that stamp court his converse. He never married, but lived in a private lodging with his sister, Grizel Weir. Many resorted to his house, to join him and hear him pray; but it was observed that he could not officiate in any holy duty without the black staff, or rod, in his hand, and leaning upon it, which made those who heard him pray admire his flood in prayer, his ready extempore expression, his heavenly gesture; so that he was thought more angel than man, and was termed by some of the holy sisters ordinarily *Angelical Thomas.*'

It is not known when Weir was overtaken by mental illness, but his activities became so bizarre that his neighbours petitioned the Lord Provost of

Edinburgh, Sir Andrew Ramsay, to have him put into custody. At length he and his sister Grizel were arrested and 'received by the magistrates'.

In his seventies now, Thomas Weir confessed, entirely of his own volition, to a long life of 'fornication, incest and sodomy' and to witchcraft in which he made special mention that he could work magic with his walking-stick. In this latter confession of witchcraft he named his sister as a witch. So Weir and his sister were brought to trial on all the counts of 'wickedness' to which he had confessed.

Nevertheless, it is clear that tender Presbyterian consciences could not stomach a charge of witchcraft in one of their most devoted supporters, so the accusations were manipulated to avoid the inference of witchcraft. Writing in *Annals of Scotland*, the law historian Lord Hailes made these points: 'Certain it is that Major Weir was neither accused nor found guilty of witchcraft; and that his sister, although accused, was not found guilty of witchcraft. The judgement of the court was adapted to the verdict, finding incest and bestiality: it says nothing of witchcraft, or of the walking-stick conjuration'.

At the trial the majority of jurors found Weir guilty and his sister was declared guilty unanimously. Weir was executed by hanging and fire at Gallowhill, Edinburgh on 14 April 1670 and his

sister was hanged in the Grassmarket at the same time.

Decades after his execution, Thomas Weir was still talked of as one of Scotland's most famous witches. His house at the Head of the Bow, West Bow, Edinburgh was famous, and Robert Chambers wrote in his *Traditions of Edinburgh* (1947):

'His house, though known to be deserted by everything human, was sometimes observed at midnight to be full of lights, and heard to emit strange sounds, as of dancing, howling, and, what is strangest of all, spinning. Some people occasionally saw the Major issue from the low close at midnight, mounted on a black horse without a lead, and gallop off in a whirlwind of flame'.

The Bargarran Imposter: The Renfrew Witches, 1697

Singled out by many as the strangest of all Scottish witchcraft cases, that of the Renfrew Witches is a classic example of a trial in which children were accusers; it is, too, a record of hysteria, ignorance, trickery, lies and imposture. It was the writer Hugo Arnot, in his *Celebrated Criminal Trials* of 1785, who called the case of Christian Shaw and the Renfrew Witches the 'Bargarran Imposter'.

The affliction of 10-year-old Christian, daughter of John Shaw, laird of Bargarran, Erskine, came to a head in 1697. For some time the child had suffered from a strange illness of fits and vomiting; during her fits she said she was tormented by 'several persons'. Christian herself traced her illness back to 17 August 1696, the day upon which she had been cursed by a 20-year-old Highland housemaid, Katherine Campbell.

Christian had accused the maid of stealing milk and had been roundly cursed with the words 'the Devil harle [drag] your soul through Hell'. Obviously frightened by the vehemence of the curse, Christian itched for revenge.

In her fits the young girl cried out that Katherine Campbell and a beggar woman, Agnes Naismith, who came regularly to Bargarran to beg, were cutting her sides. It was a story easy to make credible as Agnes Naismith was herself feared in the neighbourhood as a witch.

A number of consultations with prominent apothecaries proved fruitless and Christian Shaw was now observed to be vomiting a curious mixture of animal hair, straw and bones. She was declared bewitched and her parish minister, Andrew Turner, reported the case to his Presbytery. In turn the Presbytery considered the child's bewitchment to be serious enough to inform His Majesty's Privy Council at Edinburgh.

Matters now grew worse; Christian Shaw reputedly suffered from 'flying fits', in which she was seen flying around the house by several witnesses. On 19 January 1697 the Lords of His Majesty's Privy Council ordered a Commission to examine the case.

One by one people who were named by Christian Shaw in one of her fits as her 'tormentors' were arrested. The prisoners were examined under Alexander, 5th Lord Blantyre, as Commission President.

As the examination proceeded one accused another until 21 people were indicted, and Christian Shaw attested that they all, at one time or another and in the form of demonic spectres, had tormented her.

On 11 February 1697 a public fast day was held for Christian Shaw's 'release' from these demons. In due course the investigating Commission reported and recorded confessions including those of children related to the accused who said they had been taken to sabbats, had killed a minister there, had strangled two children (the three named had in reality been dead for some time), caused a ship to be wrecked and concocted poisons. One accuser, Elizabeth Anderson, said that she had seen her own father talking to the Devil, along with Agnes Naismith; in the child's hearing she said they had plotted to kill Christian Shaw.

The young people's hallucinations were enough for a second Commission to be authorized on 5 April 1697; this time with the power of the death sentence. The prosecution was to be led by Lord Advocate Sir James Stewart and the preliminaries opened at Renfrew Council Chamber. All the while Christian Shaw's fits demon-infested dreams and 'tormentings' had continued.

The accused now numbered 26. More examinations were made, including body searches for the 'Devil's marks'. Various 'suspicious' skin markings were noted by the 'prickers' and statements were assembled for the grand trial of the Renfrew Witches on 13 April at Paisley.

James Robertson, advocate, acted for the accused's defence and Francis Grant (later Lord Cullen) led for the prosecution with James Stewart. These men were all experienced lawyers and both sides quoted extensively from scholars on witchcraft including the much favoured (in Scottish cases) *Disquisitionum Magicarum* by the Jesuit scholar Martine Antoine Del Rio (1551–1608).

Both sides having spoken, and with all the accused questioned, the Lord Advocate warned the fifteen-strong jury that if they acquitted they 'would be accessory to all the blasphemies, apostasies, murders, tortures, and seductions, whereof these enemies of heaven and earth should be guilty'. Even though the statement was disgracefully partisan, the jury took seven hours to decide, and seven of the accused were found guilty as charged. The were burned on 10 June 1697 at Gallo Green, George St, Paisley.

Christian Shaw's fits, vomitings and hallucinations ceased after the executions. In 1718 she married a minister, John Millar of Kilmaurs, Ayrshire. After his death in 1725 she introduced machinery from Holland to make fine sewing thread, the 'Bargarran', which led to the growth of the Paisley linen thread industry. She married again in 1737, this time to the glover William Livingstone, but it is not known when she died.

In 1839 the authors Mitchell and Dickie visited the old Shaw house at Bargarran with a view to doing some field study into the case. They noted the environs of the house and the structure of its rooms and noticed a hole in the wall of what had been Christian Shaw's room. They concluded that an accomplice could have passed Christian a variety of objects to 'vomit' by sleight of hand. They commented thus in their *The Philosphy of Witchcraft* (1839): 'The clergy of Paisley and neighbouring parishes gave countenance to the murder of seven individuals in that place in 1697, and sanctified their horrid deeds by the observance of a solemn fast'.

Down the decades Christian Shaw has been portrayed both as 'victim' and 'villainess', and today it may be added that she probably suffered from a form of hysteria which produces symptoms of physical pain.

The Pittenweem Witches, 1704–5

The fishing village of Pittenweem, Fife, had recorded noteworthy witchcraft incidents in 1643–4. The families of four local witches were each made responsible for paying the expenses of executing their relatives; and the inquisitors made much of searching for 'markes of the Devil' as in the trial of Christian Roch (Laing *Lindores Abbey*). Even so the cases of 1704–5, more than many others, showed how the bigotry of ministers of the Scottish Kirk fanned the flames of persecution, inciting mob violence.

The root of the witch troubles of 1704–5 at Pittenweem was a 16-year-old youth, Patrick Morton. The case has parallels with the 'Bargarran Imposter', as was pointed out in the minutes of the Pittenweem Kirk Session, and it is apparent that the local minister had filled the youth's head with details of the Christian Shaw delusions.

During 1704 this apprentice blacksmith was asked to make a set of nails at his father's forge for Beatrix Laing, the wife of a former Treasurer of Pittenweem. Young Morton averred that he was too busy and was duly cursed by the woman. The next day Morton watched Beatrix Laing throw hot coals into water 'and knew his fate was being determined by witchcraft'.

Not long after, the young blacksmith was

incapacitated with weakness of the legs and emaciation. By the mid-months of 1704 he was showing symptoms of epilepsy and had trouble breathing. He began to make deranged accusations against Beatrix Laing and others including the wife of one Nicholas Lawson, a prominent burgess, and Janet Corphat. Morton showed to anyone he could interest the marks on his arms which he claimed had been pinched by the witches he had accused. On 19 May 1704 he informed the local minister that he would not rest easy until the witches were punished. A contemporary source records Morton's own account of one of his hallucinatory experiences: 'He said he saw Satan standing in the bed and said unto him, "My child, I will give you a silver suit and silver tressing about your hat, if you will confess that there is no Saviour; though two of my dear children [Beatrix Laing and Mrs Lawson] suffer punishment, yet it shall be well with you hereafter."'

A petition of the Scottish Privy Council of 13 June 1704 allowed for the unfortunate accused to be arrested. Beatrix Laing was cruelly tortured and she named Janet Corphat, Mrs Nicholas Lawson and Isobel Adam as her accomplices in witchcraft. When she recovered a little from the torture Beatrix Laing recanted, but was imprisoned by the Pittenweem magistrates to think again. At length the Privy Council ordered that she be released with a fine of £8. She was driven out of Pittenweem by the locals and died at St Andrews 'undesired'.

Another of the accused, Isobel Adam, was released on paying off the inquisitors in cash (she was fined illegally) and by supplying a written confession which read:

'Confess that about a fortnight after Martinmas [11 Nov], she came to Beatrix Laing's, and that she saw a little black man with a hat and black clothes, sitting at the board end, and Beatrix said: "Here is a gentleman that will fee [hire] you" . . . Upon which she engaged, and the Devil kissed her, and told her that he knew she was discontent with her lot, and that in his service she should get riches as much as she could wish. And that upon New Year's Day thereafter, the Devil appeared to her in Thomas Adam's house, and there she renounced her baptism vows; and likewise acknowledges that she was in [Andrew] Macgregor's house with Beatrix Laing, [Mrs] Nicholas Lawson, Janet Corphat, and Thomas Brown, upon a design to strangle the said Macgregor.'

The last-named Thomas Brown died in Pittenweem jail not long after his arrest.

Patrick Morton's third victim was Janet Corphat, whose torture, retrial and conviction was brought about by the youth's ramblings. This time though they were backed up by Alexander Macgregor, who was mentioned in the Isobel Adam 'confession'. In Corphat's case the Pittenweem minister, the Rev Patrick Cowper personally flogged Janet Corphat and she was put in the burgh jail. Eventually she was released as no real evidence had been brought against her.

During the night of 30 January 1705, a mob of Pittenweem folk dragged her from the house in which she was staying and took her, bruised, bleeding and bound to the beach. There she was tied to a ship's mooring hawser and stoned; half dead, the last breath was crushed out of her with heavy stones laid on her chest. In his *Tracts on Witchcraft* (1677) John Webster writes: 'And to be sure it was [that she was dead], they called a man with a horse and a sledge, and made him drive over her corpse backward and forward several times'. The Rev Cowper made no attempt to intervene and denied her Christian burial in Pittenweem kirkyard; none of the mob were prosecuted for Janet Corphat's murder.

After the turn of the 18th century witch accusations began to tail off, but superstition leading to executions still remained throughout Scotland from Selkirk (Meg Lawson) to Shetland (Barbara Tulloch and Ellen King) and from Anstruther-Easter (Elspeth Dick) to Inverness (George and Lachlan Rattray).

On 3 May 1709, in a trial at Dumfries, Elspeth Rule became the last person tried in the Court of

Judiciary on a general charge that she was by 'habit and repute a witch'. Hugo Arnot in his *Criminal Trials* (1785) wrote of her sentence: 'The jury, by a majority of voices, found these articles [that she had used threatening expressions against persons at enmity with her, who were afterwards visited with the loss of cattle, or the death of friends] proved, and the Judge ordained the prisoner to be burned on the cheek, and to be banished Scotland for life'.

At Dornoch, Sutherland, the last legal trial for witchcraft in Scotland took place during June 1727. The trial was of Janet Horne and her daughter, although the daughter ultimately escaped. Sheriff-depute Captain David Ross of Little Dean heard the accusations which included the claim that 'among other crimes [she had] ridden upon her own daughter, transformed into a pony, and shod by the Devil, which made the girl ever after lame, both in hands and feet, a misfortune entailed upon [the daughter's] son'. So wrote Charles Kirkpatrick Sharpe (1781–1851), a prominent Scottish witchcraft chronicler, in his *Witchcraft in Scotland* (1884). Janet Horne was found guilty and executed in a burning pitch barrel, and for decades afterwards members of her family were still reviled by the folk of Sutherland.

During 1736, the 1604 *Act Anentis Witchcraft* was repealed and Scotland's law concerning witchcraft was brought into line with that of England.

It is difficult today to estimate the number of witches executed during the years of witch mania in Scotland. Executions were patchy in their intensity over the country, and during Cromwell's occupation of Scotland (1651–60) witch persecution almost ceased. Yet in 1661, in one month alone, 120 women were executed as witches according to naturalist John Ray (1627–1705).

There have been many wild guesses as to the number of witches executed in Scotland. Charles Mackay in his *Memoirs of Extraordinary Popular Delusions* (1841) sets the figure at 17 000 between the passing of Mary's Act in 1563 and the accession of James VI to the throne of England in 1603. Again,

Robert Steele in an essay in *Social England* (1903) puts the deaths at 8 000 between 1560 and 1600. From the evidence of official records and casual mentions of witchcraft in diaries and journals, an estimate of 4 400 executions from 1510 to 1727 is likely to be nearer the mark.

The Devil and All His Works

This night in my sleep I was aghast,
Me thought the Devil was tempting fast,
The people, with aiths of crueltie;
Saying, as through the mercat he past,
Renunce thy God, and cum to me.
The Devil's Inquest William Dunbar (c1456–1513)

The witch hunters and trial inquisitors of Scotland were always anxious to find evidence that the hand of the Devil was behind the activities of the country's supposed witches. To prove that the Devil was involved was a key factor in securing an indictment; legal recognition was therefore sought that the Devil was the supreme master of witches, and a person resourceful and cunning because of his great experience in bedevilling Christians 'almoste of sixe thousands yeares' said one chronicler.

Thinking of the Pittenweem Witch cruelties the antiquary Thomas George Stevenson wrote in 1871, citing the local minister as a frontline seeker-out of supposed Devil worship: 'In places where the minister was inflamed with holy zeal against the Devil and his emissaries, the parish became a perfect hotbed for the rearing of witches; and so plentiful a crop did it produce, that it appeared nothing else could thrive. But in places where the minister had some portion of humanity, and a little common sense, the Devil very rarely set foot on his territories, and witchcraft was not to be found'.

The acceptance of the Devil is firmly attested in Scottish history and literature. Scotland has a rich proverbial lore about the Devil. Here are a few examples:

The Devil seems to be God to somebody.
The Devil is not always at one door.

He needs a lang-shanket spoon that sups kail wi' the Deil.
If it rains while the sun is shining the Devil is beating his grandmother; he is laughing and she is crying.
Playing cards are the Devil's prayer book.
'Twas surely the Devil who taught women to dance and asses to pray.
The Devil makes his dinner out of lawyers' tongues and ministers' fingers.
A wicked woman and an evil is three bawbees worse than the Devil.
Man, woman and the Devil are three degrees of comparison.
The Devil lies brooding in the miser's chest.

No other nation has Scotland's wealth of nicknames for the Devil: Auld Clootie, Auld Chiel, Auld Harry, Auld Sandy, Plotcock and the Earl of Hell are all Lowland names, while in the Highlands and Islands he is also known as the Big Brindled One and *Muc Mhor Dhubh* (Big Black Pig). It was, of course, a Highland superstition that the natural markings on pigs' trotters were the 'Devil's Marks' and that anyone eating pork would contract a deadly disease.

Various parts of Scotland are identified as the Evil One's own: the Devil's Staircase is found at Glencoe; The Devil's Cauldron at Lednock River, Perthshire; the Devil's Elbow at Braemar and the Devil's Beeftub at Moffat are a few examples. In Skye can be found his church, the *Eaglais Bhrcigie*, and his pulpit, the *Cubaid*. Parts of the Devil's dwelling are more precisely pinpointed: the chimney of his house, Hell's Lum, is located at Pennan, a fishing village in Aberdeenshire.

Local Scottish historical lore has woven the Devil's thread into its tapestry. The Devil, for instance, is said by Sir John Sinclair of Ulbster, preparer of *The Statistical Account of Scotland* (1791–9), to have abducted Patrick Forbes, Bishop of Aberdeen, from his castle at Craigievar, leaving his footprints on the gable end of the castle. S Cowan in *The Royal House of Stuart* (1908) repeats the story of how the reformer John Knox is said to have conversed with the Devil in the cathedral churchyard of St Andrews, and, according to the *State Trials* (1816), the Devil is recounted as having appeared to a man called Williamson, a schoolmaster at Coupar Angus, in 1678.

The Devil of the Scots witchcraft inquisitors was not the horned god of Celtic legend, but the Christian Satan, as quoted by Scottish clerics from Isaiah: 'How art thou fallen from heaven, O Lucifer, son of the morning'. Satan, whose recognizable form emerges in Job with the prime duty of tempting man in many guises, was a 'person' in Scotland by the Middle Ages.

While they were at it the Scots invented their own diabology. Not for them were the incubi, succubi, xorguinae or bruxae of the Franciscan Alphonsus de Spina's *Fortalicium Fidei* (Fortress of the Faith, 1459), read in cloister and manse, nor the ancient kindly 'faerie folk' of English folklore. In Scotland they had fell goblins, brownies of gruesome shape, spunkies of hurtful mein, luring kelpies and foul moulachs alternately haunting the trackless hills and harsh stone lochsides. In Scotland, too, the 'little people' were not the elves and fairies of 'Albion Glades', but distinctive, homegrown demons from Hell.

Scotland's Devil is by no means uniform in appearance to his devotees. Borderland folklore said that he was able to turn himself into a black ram with fiery eyes, a sow, a bull, a goat, a horse, a large black dog or a brindled cat at will. And in a half-animal, half-human form his image is most often 'ane meikle black man' (that is, of swarthy complexion) as in the Alexander Hamilton witch trial held at Haddington in 1629; or a 'rough tanny hound' as in the William Barton trial at Edinburgh, 1655.

In no other country did the Devil appear in so many tradesmens' guises than in Scotland: blacksmith, carpenter, cobbler, farmer, musician, fisherman, soldier, tailor, tinker and dark-suited kirk elder. But most popular of all was the Devil Weaver of popular ballad:

The weaver de'il gaed out at night
To see the new, new moon,
Wi' a' the traddles at his back,
An' the sowin' bag aboon.

All this conformed with the Kirk's teachings about the Devil, named Legion, who entered the Gadarene swine in Mark's gospel account.

A key factor in Scottish witchcraft superstition and witch trials was the supposed 'Pact with the Devil', in which essentially the witch agreed to work with and for the Devil against humanity and the Christian God. The witchlore writer George Gifford (d1620) spelled it out for the Reformed clergy in his *Discourse of the Subtle Practices of Devils by Witchcraft* (1587): 'A witch by the word of God ought to die the death not because she killeth man—for that she cannot, unless it be those witches which kill by poison, which either they receive from the Devil, or he teacheth them to make—but because she dealeth with devils'.

To give academic credibility to witch prosecution documents Scots inquisitors often included in witch 'confessions' a Latin pact. This is an example of what the witch would be supposed to sign:

Domine magisterque Lucifer te deum et principem agnosco, et polliceor tibi servire et obedire quandiu potero vivere.

[My lord and master Lucifer, I acknowledge thee as my God and prince, and promise to serve and obey thee as long as I shall live.]
Et renuncio alterum Deum et Jesum Christum et alios sanctos atque sanctas et Ecclesiam Scotam et omnia ipsius sacramenta et omnes orationes et rogationes quibus fideles possint intercedere pro me.
[And I renounce the other God, as well as Jesus Christ, all the saints, the Scottish church, all the sacraments, and all the prayers and petitions by which the faithful might intercede for me].
Et tibi policeor quid faciam quotquot malum potero, et attrahere ad mala per omnes.
[And I promise thee that I will do as much evil as I can, and that I will draw everyone else to evil].
Et abrenuncio chrismam et baptismum, et omnia merita Jesu Christi et ipsius sanctorum.
[I renounce chrism, baptism, all the merits of Jesus Christ and his saints.]
Et sideero tuae servitui et adorationi, et si non oblationem mei ipsius fecero, ter quoque die, tibi do vitam meam sicut tuam.
[And if I fail to serve and adore thee, and if I do not pay thee homage thrice a day, I give you my life as thine own.]

The whole, given a Romish overtone for good measure, was signed (or forged) in the witch's name with the sentiment *Extractum ex infernis* [Extracted from Hell] added.

Rewards expected for such pacts varied in witch superstition, but in Major Weir's trial of 1670, his witch sister was granted a 'familiar spirit' which span for her 'in a shorter time than three or four women could have done the same'.

The Devil, in Scottish clerical circles, was thought to baptize his converts by means of a mock baptism ceremony (after the renunciation of the Christian baptism as set out in the Pact) and the giving of a new witch name; such a ritual was quoted in the Margaret McIllivein trial of 1662 at Bute and recounted in *Highland Papers*. After the baptism the Devil was thought to mark his converts with 'the Devil's Claw', so such blemishes as birthmarks, freckles, moles and other scars were singled out as clues in identifying possible witches. In 1658 eleven women and two men were accused of witchcraft at Alloa. One of their number, Margaret Taylor, attested that the Devil 'in the likeness of a young man with gray clothes and a blue cap . . . gave her his mark . . . in her secret member'.

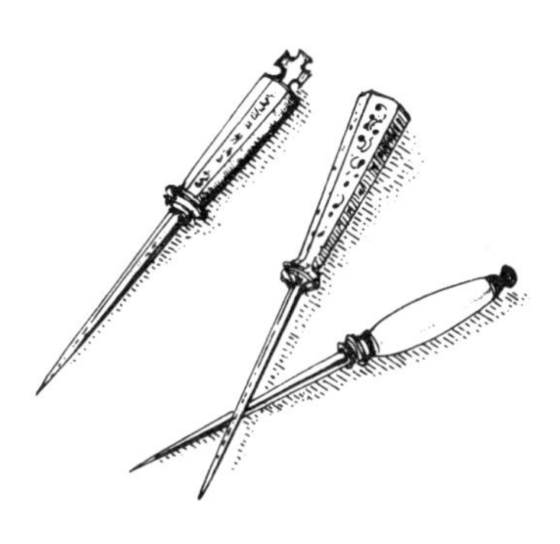

The inquisitors deemed these *stigmata diaboli* (Devil's Marks) or *sigillum diaboli* (Devil's Seals) to be insensible to pain, and if pricked they would not bleed. So Scotland's witchfinders carried long sharp bodkins to probe the blemishes by pricking; in Scotland these witchfinders were called 'prickers'. Some such were local burgh employees, as witness the Dumfries Treasurer's wage payments to one Thomas Crawford. Other 'professionals' included John Kinaird of Tranent, John Balfour of Corhouse and John Dick. They often had a roving commission to 'prick' as the historian Ralph Gardiner testified in 1655: 'When the sergeants had brought [the pricker] . . . to the town, the magistrates sent their bellman through the town . . . crying: All that would bring in any complaint against any woman for a witch, they should be sent for and tried by the person appointed . . . women were brought . . . and stripped, and then had pins thrust into their bodies'. John Balfour, however, showed too much zeal in his 'pricking' and the Scottish Privy Council forbade him to 'practise his trade' as he was 'abusing simple and ignorant people for his private gain'.

The finding of such a presumed satanic mark was cause enough in Scotland for a prosecution for witchcraft. David Vedder noted this in *The Witch of Pittenweem:*

> And the more to prove her allegiance true,
> Like as vassal gude an' leal,
> She had branded her banes wi' Sathan's mark,
> And her flesh his privy seal.

Scottish witchlore threw up several other delusions about the Devil: the Devil's Ground was one which persisted. People believed that certain parts of the countryside belonged to the Devil, and that to try to cultivate them meant death by cursing. These plots were termed 'The Guid Man's Crofts' and were left over to tares and weeds. In the Border shires they went further; certain portions of the town glebe were deliberately left uncultivated as a sop to the Devil; the plots were called 'Clootie's Crofts'.

The Devil played no less a part in Scottish superstition. He was given his own day, Friday. No one liked to transact business on a Friday lest the Devil interfere. Likewise Friday was an unlucky day on which to get married, or to set out on a journey, and to sneeze on a Friday was said to attract the Devil's attention.

The Scots even gave the Devil his own set of colours. A Gaelic poem from the Isle of Jura gives details:

> Dhlura an deamhain
> Agus din dathan
> an deamhain ann
> Buidhe, Dubh's Riach.
> [Jura of the Devil
> And of the colours
> of the Devil there
> Yellow, black and striped.]

'Flying demons' are often mentioned at Scottish witch trials as the 'Devil's Acolytes'. The most famous case involving them was that of Andrew Mackie from Ringfoot of Stocking, Kirkcudbrightshire. The assailing of Mackie by such demons was attested to by Rev Andrew Telfair and became a *cause célèbre* of 1695. Sir Walter Scott used the phenomenon in his book *Woodstock* and many official documents mentioned such demons too; witness the case of Captain Douglas who, while recruiting in Jedburgh, was assailed by 'furious devils armed with pitchforks'.

It has been seen that in pre-Reformation Scotland the medieval Church was more interested in hunting down heresy against its teachings than in the supposed magic conjuring of witchcraft. After the Reformation this attitude was to change in clerical circles, as the Bible was interpreted more literally and direct gospel texts pushed aside religious philosophy from the pulpits.

Theologically the predominant Scottish Devil of the country's witchcraft history was the Calvinist concept: 'an enemie that is in courage most hardie, in strength most mightie, in policies most subtle, in diligence and celeritie unweariable, with all sorts of engins plenteously furnished in skill of warre . . .' Yet when it came to witch trials the inquisitors, clerical and lay, required that the Devil be seen to be ubiquitous in all regions of Presbyterian Christendom, so the classification of the six varieties of devil set out in 1608 by Friar Francesco-Maria Guazzo in *Compendium Maleficarum* was much referred to in Scots examinations of witches even though it was done in a covert way. Here is Guazzo's classification which exactly fitted what Scotland's witch hunters believed (note that he talks in the plural):

'The first is *fiery*, because these dwell in the upper air and will never descend to the lower regions until the day of Judgement, and they have no dealings on earth with men. [Thus could the rising souls of the dead be attacked on their way to heaven].

'The second is the *aerial,* because these dwell in the air around us. They can descend to hell, and, by forming bodies out of the air, can at times be visible to men. Very frequently, with [the Master's] permission they agitate the air and raise storms and tempests, and all this they conspire to do for the destruction of mankind. [Witches raising tempests on land and sea was a common superstition.]

'The third is *terrestrial,* and these were certainly cast from Heaven to earth for their sins. Some of them live in woods and forests, and lay snares for hunters; some dwell in the fields and lead night travellers astray; some dwell in the hidden places and caverns; while others delight to live in secret among men.

'The fourth is *aqueous,* for these dwell under the water in rivers and lakes, and are full of anger, turbulent, unquiet, and deceitful. They raise storms at sea, sink ships in the ocean, and destroy life in the water. When such devils appear, they are more often women than men, for they live in moist places and lead an easier life. But those which live in drier and harder places are usually seen as males.

'The fifth is the *subterranean,* for these live in caves and caverns in the mountains. They are of a very mean disposition, and chiefly molest those who work in pits and mines for treasure, and they are always ready to do harm. They cause earthquakes and winds and fires, and shake the foundations of houses.

'The sixth is the *heliophobic,* because they especially hate and detest the light, and never appear during daytime, nor can they assume a bodily form until night.'

Guazzo said that this sixth manifestation of the Devil was the one which witches could not ape; it was one that they could not conjure up to do their will, as it was the hellish guard of the Devil himself.

Scotland's witch inquisitors had recourse to a ritual to detect if a corpse had been attacked by the Devil. For they said whenever a supposed witch was brought near to a bewitched cadaver it would bleed. This ritual was called 'Bier Rite' (or 'Right') and was a superstitious survival of the primitive 'ordeal' whereby an accused person would be tested by lot, water, fire and so on to establish guilt.

'Bier Rite' was known in Scotland as early as the 12th century for detecting demons and appears in the Dalkeith Witch Trial of 3 August 1661, concerning Elspeth Graham, Christian Patterson and Christine Wilson. According to the trial documents, the latter, protesting her innocence, 'refused to come nigh the corpse or to touch it, saying that she never touched a dead corpse in her life. But being earnestly desired by the minister and bailiffs . . . that she would touch the corpse softly, she granted to do it . . . she touching the wound of the dead man very softly, it being white and clean without any spot of blood or the like, yet immediately, while her finger was upon it, the blood rushed out of it to the great admiration [astonishment] of all beholders, who took it as a discovery of the [witch] murder'. A verdict of guilty was entered.

One writer who did more than many to defuse superstition about the supposed reality of the Devil was Robert Burns. He honoured the Devil in a number of poems like his *Address to Belzebub* (1786). Burns took the Devil of the Kirk of Scotland and humanized him as a figure of fun thus endeavouring to kill off the fear superstition inculcated. In his *Address to the Deil* (1785–6) Burns invokes the Devil and ties him in with the witches of superstition:

> O Thou! whatever title suit thee—
> Auld Hornie, Satan, Nick, or Clootie—
> Wha in yon cavern grim and sootie,
> Close under hatches,
> Spairges about the brunstane cootie,
> *splashes brimstone dish*
> To scaud poor wretches! . . . *scald*
>
> Let warlocks grim, an' wither'd hags,
> Tell how wi' you, on ragweed nags,

They skim the muirs an' dizzy crags,
Wi' wicked speed;
And in kirkyards renew their leagues,
Owre howkit dead. *exhumed*

And in saying farewell Burns gives hope for himself and humanity to escape the Devil's powers:

And now, Auld Clootie, I ken ye're thinkin,
A certain Bardie's rantin, drinkin, *roistering*
Some luckless hour will send him linkin *hurrying*
To your black pit;
But, faith! he'll turn a corner jinkin, *dodging*
An' cheat you yet!

Burns made the Devil more manageable and his name was no longer whispered with terror. In fact there was a whole flood of 'Devil' ballads and poems. James Grant (1822–87) even added something about the old superstition that one could get rid of the Devil by throwing house coals at him. Here's how Grant phrased it in *Harry Ogilvie:*

The deil sat suppin' the auld wife's kail *broth*
With a hey sing ho, and a tow, row, row!
But she raxed a het coal to the neuk o' his tail, *reached*
And loudly screiched he at the scutherin' lowe! *scorching flame*

He girned, he growled, he gabbered and grat, *moaned/wept*
With a hey sing ho, and a tow, row, row!
And doun on the ingle he shivered the pat, *pot*
And flew up the lum wi' his tail in a lowe! *chimney*

One classic 'Devil' tale portraying the Devil as roistering companion, emerged from Scottish witchlore to exhibit the popular superstitions of the day.

The Devil and Tam Dalyell

The 17th century House of the Binns, West Lothian, was built by the Edinburgh merchant Thomas Dalyell and was inherited by his son General Tam Dalyell (c1599–1685). After a succession of military appointments Tam Dalyell joined the royalist expedition that ended with the Battle of Worcester in 1651. Escaping from the Tower of London he saw foreign service in Russia fighting for the Tsar, but at the Restoration of the Stuarts, Charles II gave him command of the army in Scotland. He raised the Royal Scots Greys in 1681.

Because of his rumbustious and eccentric personality, Dalyell was made into a larger-than-life figure in common parlance and was soon to be talked of as an associate of the Devil. The story is repeated even in the most academic of architectural works that when General Tam built a new range onto the Dalyell home the Devil threatened to blow down the walls. The general replied: 'I will build me a turret at every corner to pin down my walls', which explains the toy fort aspect of the present day house.

During his lifetime, according to popular lore, General Tam often played cards with the Devil; the Devil usually won. On one occasion however the old soldier won and the Devil threw the table upon which they were playing at the general's head; the table flew out of the window into a stretch of water known as the Sergeant's Pond. Lo and behold—the superstitious were hardly surprised —when it was drained in 1878 a heavy table of carved marble was found in the mud at the pool's bottom.

Sabbats and Feasts

This nicht is Hallowe'en Janet,
The morn is Hallowday;
And, gin ye daur your true luve win,
Ye hae nae time to stay.
Tamlane

Did the medieval witches of Scotland really forgather in a common ritual of dance and magic? The truth is debatable. Superstition, however, was clear that they did, and there were eight great 'witch' celebrations cited by those who purported to know. Several of these were grafted on to the Christian calendar to make up the 'Scottish Witches' Calendar of Feasts'.

February Eve, Candlemas (1 February)
The Spring Equinox (20 March)
May Eve (30 April)
The Summer Solstice, or Midsummer (21 June)
August Eve, Lammas (31 July)
The Autumn Equinox (20 September)
Hallowe'en (31 October)
The Winter Solstice, Festival of Rebirth (20 December)

(The solstices are the times when the sun reaches its maximum distances from the equator, while the equinoxes occur when the sun crosses the equator, making night equal in length to the day.)

It is undoubted that the February, May, August and October ceremonies had some connection, in race memory at least, with the Ancient Gaelic Year and corresponded with the festivals of Beltane (1 May), Lugnasadh (20 September), Samhuin (1 November) and Imbolc (Spring). Thus the so-called 'Scottish Witch Calendar' had a very close resemblance to the northern tribal cycles of seeding, harvesting and animal procreation; to the superstitious these were all times when spirits walked the earth and mankind was vulnerable to witches and their master the Devil.

From the year 1484, in the records of Scottish witch history, there can be traced the evolvement of two main types of witch meeting. First was the periodic *esbat,* which all local witches were thought to attend, and secondly the *sabbat,* usually said to occur four or five times a year. In many later accounts, the *sabbat* is misnamed 'Witches' Sabbath', although it had no Christian connotation; the clergy, keen to involve those accused of witchcraft in heresy, deliberately substituted 'Sabbath' for *sabbat* and promoted the idea that at such feasts witches enacted a parody of the Christian liturgy.

In due time the witch hunters and inquisitors of Scotland formulated a five-part ceremonial for a witch *sabbat* which was based purely on their imaginations. First came the *Convocation.* Superstition had it that witches met when and where they liked, but usually at night. In his *Discoverie of Witchcraft* (1584), Reginald Scot says they met in certain situations: 'As for the places of magical circles, they are to be chosen melancholy, doleful, dark and lonely; either in Woods or Deserts, or amongst ruins of Castles, Abbeys, Monasteries,

&c, or upon the seashore when the Moon shines clear, or else in some large Parlour hung with black and the floors covered with the same, with doors and windows closely shut, and waxen candles lighted'.

In Scottish witch-lore a crossroads, or better still a meeting of three roads or paths, was a good place for witches to gather, as was a spot beside a sinister-looking tree or a strangely-shaped boulder. How they arrived varied too, from broomstick to catback, but in many places in Scotland it was believed that witches arrived at their great feasts as if they were cavalry. This we can see in the traditional rallying song of the witches from Galloway:

> Up horses a, but mair adowe!
> Ryde, ryde for Lochar-brig-knowe!

The clerics of Scotland were precise in defining the sabbat, or coven as it was more commonly called, as a secret nightly conventicle in which 12 male or female witches gathered together while a thirteenth aped the Devil; until such times, of course, that the Master deigned to make a personal appearance. This was clearly the medieval and reformed Church's attempts to underline a deliberate blasphemy of the thirteen present at the Last Supper with Jesus, as is remembered in the old Scots adage, 'Thirteen—The Devil's Dozen'.

The first recorded mention of a sabbat, or coven, in Scotland is to be found in the trial of Elizabeth 'Bessie' Dunlop of Lyne, Ayrshire on 8 November 1576. Dunlop's confession is detailed in *Criminal Trials* and she claimed to have met the ghost of a male witch called Thomas Reid, who in reality had been killed at the Battle of Pinkie in 1547. Reid, she said, encouraged here to become a witch and join in covens.

At the trial of Isobel Smyth at Forfar in 1661, recorded in the *Register of the Privy Council,* there is the first mention of the 'great feast covens' of the witches at Candlemas (2 February), May Eve (30

April), Lammas (1 August) and Hallowe'en (31 October).

The records of Scottish witch confessions at trials talk much of the supposed initiation ceremonies into witchcraft which usually took place in churchyards, ruined churches or consecrated ground.

The ceremonies usually concerned the renunciation of Christian baptism and the beginning of a new pact with Satan, with the promise to follow 'His Dark Majesty' and worship him as a true god. In return Satan marked the participants with a secret symbol on some hidden part of their skin. Such a process was described in the trial of Janet Boyd, wife of Robert Neill, burgess of Dumbarton in 1628.

A rebaptism took place after renunciation and the converts were given a witch name. For instance, at the Bute case of 1662, Margaret McIllivein told how she had been renamed Janet. More imaginatively ridiculous names were given to the Auldearn witches of the same year: Bessie Wilson was renamed 'Throw-the-Cornyard', and Jane Mairton 'Over-the-Dyke-with-it'. (The latter, incidentally, referred to a leaping dance similar to the one danced to 'Owre the lave o't', which Robert Burns used as an air for his 'Whistle owre the lave o't'.) This new naming was an apeing of the medieval Church's ceremony of taking a new name at the first confirmation Mass.

After the *convocation* came the *veneration*. Many a witch trial in Scotland heard how witches made some sort of allegiance to the Devil at sabbats. Sometimes this is mentioned as a 'marriage' to Satan, sealed with the *osculum infame* ('kiss of shame') for the leader of the group. Then came the *manducation*.

This was pictured as an orgy of gluttony. In the *Reliquiae Antiquae Scoticae* (1848), G R Kinloch mentions the Elspet Alexander case in which specific foods were mentioned, 'flesh, bread, and aile', while a sister-witch Elspet Bruce offered the Devil a goose at a gathering in her house which gave her 'great favour with her master'. Food was made in the witches' cauldron for the coven after the magic potions had been made; sometimes a witch dumpling, bannock or cake was made to ape the Mass bread. Robert Hartley Cromeck found this comment about the witch bannock in the lore of south-west Scotland and noted it in his *Memoirs of Nithsdale and Galloway:*

> She hynt them a' in her mou' and chowed, *gathered up*
> She hynt them a' in her mou' and chowed,
> She drabbled them owre wi' a black tade's blude,
> And baked a bannock—and ca'd it gude.

Food was followed by the *celebration,* when the witches danced 'in the form of a circle and always to the left'. The trial records show that the dance was led, conga-style, by the coven leader around a prehistoric stone, or a mercat cross like the one described in the Thomas Leyis case at Aberdeen of 1596. Indeed Reginald Scott in his *Discoverie of Witchcraft* (1584) even averred that the modern waltz developed from its origin in the witch dance to become *La Volta.* In the 1597 Janet Lucas case at Aberdeen, the representative of the Devil sat in the centre of the circle and played for the dancers.

In 1939, *Chambers Journal* recorded fragments of a traditional song said to have been sung by North Berwick witches in 1630 as they danced a reel:

> Cummer gae ye afore, cummer ga ye,
> Gin ye winna gae afore, cummer let me,

Ring-a-ring a-widdershins
Whirlin', skirlin', widdershins
And Deil tak the hinnermaist
Whae'er she be!

The coven or sabbat was completed with the *copulation,* a factor particularly noted in the North Berwick witch trials of 1630 and 1663.

Writing in his *Witchcraft and Demonology* (1959), Rossell Hope Robbins commented: 'According to the confessions extracted from witches by the courts, women attending sabbats always had sexual intercourse with the Devil. Theologians accepted the reality of intercourse between humans and the Devil, either as a male incubus or as a female succubus, and debated on the nature of the devils (whether corporeal or spirit), the extent of the sin, and the techniques of the act'.

Several Popes, such as Innocent VIII and Benedict XIV in his *De Servorum Dei Beatificatione,* agreed that sexual intercourse with demons was possible, quoting such authorities as St Augustine. This line of thought was picked up by the clerics of Scotland's Reformed Church and thereafter sexual overtones entered all Scots trials from 1559.

Scots cases featuring male witches have few mentions of sexual relations with devils; interest undoubtedly centred on women with local ministers, sheriffs and burgesses paying a prurient attention.

Before they were executed in 1679, the witches of Bo'ness, West Lothian confessed intimacy with the Devil. The confession is quoted in *Criminal Trials,* and tells how the Devil 'would have carnal dealing with [them] in the shape of a deer, or in any other shape, now and then. Sometimes he would be like a stork, a bull, a deer, a roe, or a dog, and have dealing with [them]'. One of the six Bo'ness witches, Margaret Hamilton, was accused of having had 'carnal copulation with the Devil in the likeness of a man, but he removed from [her] in the likeness of a black dog'. And at her trial in

1662 Isobel Gowdie of Auldearne confessed that she 'found [the Devil's] "nature" as cold within [her] as spring well water'.

There were, of course, a number of anti-witch feasts held at certain times. For instance, the Feast of St John the Baptist (24 June) was considered by superstitious Scots burghers as a good time to take out insurance against witches. Bonfires were lit to drive witchcraft away for a twelvemonth, particularly at Bressay Sound, Shetland.

For the folk of Aberdeenshire, Beltane was the time to counter witches as they rode through stackyards to steal milk and meal. As the children danced around the bonfires they would shout 'Gie's a peat to burn the witches', and as the last flames flickered all said 'De'il tak the hindmost'.

Above all others was the great 'Witch Feast' of Hallowe'en, or All Hallowmass Eve (31 October) as it was called in pre-Reformation times. Before 1559 the Scottish Church remembered the blessed dead at this feast, but long before Christianity had influenced Scotland the tribesmen had averred that at this time the doors between life and death swung open and the spirits of the dead poured out to visit the mortal places they had known.

The children who danced through the Victorian and Edwardian streets of Scotland with their candlelit hollowed-out turnips in the shape of grimacing faces were commemorating this prehistoric spirit visitation. The turnip lanterns were a relic of the animal and human skulls stuck on poles at the edge of tribal villages to keep the spirits away.

By the 17th and 18th centuries Scots folk believed that Hallowe'en was a time when the demons of earth, water, fire and air were particularly active, all under the command of the greatest witch of all, the Nighthag. Sir Walter Scott gave this awesome creature life in his book *Waverley:*

> On Hallowmas Eve, e'er ye boune to rest,
> Ever beware that your couch be blest;
> Sign it with cross and sain it with bead.
> Sing the Ave and the Creed.
> For on Hallowmas Eve the Nighthag shall ride,
> And all her nine-fold sweeping on by her side,
> Whether the wind sing lowly or loud,
> Sailing through moonshine or swathed in a cloud.

And so the Nighthag and her band winged through the night to a lonely spot or ruined church to dance their Hallowe'en steps. Robert Burns used the old Ayrshire superstition in his *Tam o'Shanter* to recreat this dance:

> . . . glimmering through the groaning trees,
> Kirk Alloway seemed in a bleeze:
> Through ilka bore the beams were glancing,
> And loud resounding mirth and dancing . . .
> Warlocks and witches in a dance:
> Nae cotillion, brent new frae France,
> But hornpipes, jigs, strathspeys, and reels,
> Put life and mettle at their heels.
> A winnock-bunker in the east,
> There sat Auld Nick, in shape o'beast;
> A touzie tyke, black, grim and large,
> Tae gie them music was his charge:
> He screw'd the pipes and gart them skirl,
> Till roof and rafters a' did dirl.

Yes, it was all true, the old folk said, for had not the Aberdeen witches of 1596 attested that they had so danced around the mercat cross at Hallowe'en, and further jigged around the 'grey stane' at the foot of the hill at Craigleuch?

In his poetic celebration of Hallowe'en Robert

Burns dwelt on several aspects of divination. Burns took a great deal of interest in witchcraft and the supernatural, and credited his knowledge and interest to 'an old maid of my Mother's'. He wrote in 1787 to Dr John Moore that: 'She [Betty Davidson] had, I suppose, the largest collection in the county of tales and songs concerning devils, ghosts, fairies, brownies, witches, warlocks, spunkies, kelpies, elf candles, dead-lights, wraiths, apparitions, cantraips, giants, inchanted towers, dragons and other trumpery'.

So it was Betty's tales that gave Burns the folkloric basis for his *Hallowe'en*. He wrote this explanation for the poem in 1786: '[Hallowe'en] is thought to be a night when witches, Devils, and other mischief-making beings are abroad on their baneful, midnight errands; particularly those aerial people, the Fairies, are said, on that night, to hold a grand Anniversary'.

In *Hallowe'en* Burns noted down all the Hallowe'en customs extant in his day. 'Upon that night, when Fairies light,' he wrote, folk gathered in various parts of Carrick:

> To burn their nits, an' pou their stocks, *nuts*
> And haud their Hallowe'en.

Burns himself added this note of explanation about the 'stocks':

'The first ceremony of Hallowe'en, is, pulling each a *Stock*, or plant of kail. They must go out, hand in hand, with eyes shut, and pull the first they meet with: its being big or little, straight or crooked, is prophetic of the size and shape of the grand object of their Spells—the husband or wife. If any yird, or earth, stick to the root, that is tocher, or fortune; and the taste of the custoc, that is the heart of the stem, is indicative of the natural temper and disposition. Lastly, the stems, or to give them their ordinary appellation, the runts, are placed somewhere above the head of the door; and the Christian names of the people whom chance brings into the house, are, according to the priority of placing the runts, the names in question'. Thus could the name and personality of a future spouse be divined.

Burns then goes on to the next ploy:

> The lasses staw frae 'mang them a'
> To pou their stalks o'corn.

for which he wrote this explanation:

'They go to the barnyard, and pull each, at three several times, a stalk of oats. If the third stalk wants the top-pickle, that is, the grain at the top of the stalk, the party in question will want the maidenhead'.

So it was prophesied that the puller or the future spouse would not be a virgin on marriage. Then came the popular nut charm ceremony:

> The auld Guidwife's weel-hoorded nits,
> Are round and round divided . . .
> Some kindle couthie side by side . . .
> Some start awa, wi' saucy pride . . .

Burns then describes how the Christian name and surname of a future spouse can be identified by throwing a thread of blue yarn into the brewing pot of the family kiln. When it comes out the thread will be twisted into the form of initials.

Some girls preferred this alternative divination:

> We Jenny to her Graunie says,
> 'Will ye go wi' me Graunie?
> I'll eat the apple at the glass,
> I gat frae Uncle Johnie.'

Burns explained, too, what this was about: 'Take a candle, and go, alone to a looking glass: eat an apple before it, and some traditions say you should comb your hair all the time: the face of your conjugal companion, to be, will be seen in the glass, as if peeping over your shoulder'.

Burns finishes off his tale with the ceremony of the 'Luggies' for which he gives this account:

'Take three dishes; put clean water into one, foul water in another, and leave the third empty: blindfold a person, and lead him to the hearth where the dishes are ranged; he (or she) dips the left hand: if by chance in the clean, the future husband or wife will come to the bar of matrimony, a maid; if in the foul, a widow; if in the empty dish, it foretells, with equal certainty, no marriage at all. It is repeated three times; and every time the arrangement of the dishes is altered'.

Burns was quoting but a few acts of divination that were still extant in the Scotland of his day. But from the 17th century in Scotland the list of witch divinations was expanded in the cognizance of Scotland's witch hunters who believed—or purported to believe—that witches carried out a comprehensive programme of divinations at their sabbats.

By legal definition the crime which witches committed when they took part in divination was one of deception, the law taking no account of the evil nature of the means employed. Nevertheless, Scots witch persecutors were keen to prove the evil ambience of divination whether it be naive nature worship (divination from herbs) or deluded satanism (calling up demons to assist).

The witch hunters perceived divination to have two main parts: the spell and the rite. In spell-making the witch uttered the words of a magic formula, and then came the rite, a mime to transfer the power of the spell into objects. Thus in the minds of witch hunters a harmless gesturing to bring rain to parched fields was just as evil as dancing at a sabbat in honour of the Devil.

In due time the writer John Gaule in his

Mysmantia (1652) made it easy for witch hunters to give some academic credibility to the understanding of witch divination by listing the various methods of divination with their own vocabulary:

Aeromancy divining by the air and weather vanes.

Alectryomancy by roosters and poultry; their actions.

Alphitomancy by meal, flour and bran in bowl or girnal.

Antinopomancy by the entrails of victims.

Arithmancy by numbers.

Astragalomancy by dice, or gaming tokens.

Axinomancy by saws and cutting edges; how they were marked.

Botanomancy by herbs; growth, wilting and colours.

Capnomancy by smoke; how it rose and dispersed.

Carromancy by melting wax; candle-drips and wick-burning.

Catoxtromancy by looking-glasses.

Cattabomancy by vessels of brass and other metals.

Cephalonomancy by broiling of an ass's or a sheep's head.

Chartomancy by writing in papers. Handwriting.

Chiromancy by the lines on the hand. Palmistry.

Cleromancy by drawing lots.

Coscinomancy by sieves. The study of residues.

Crithomancy by grain or corn. Texture, growth, colour.

Crystallomancy by drinking glasses. Reading lees.

Dactylomancy by rings. Jewellery.

Demonomancy by the suggestion of evil demons.

Gastromancy by the sound of or signs on the belly (or in large-bellied glasses)

Geomancy by soil and stones.

Gyromancy by rounds or circles, drawn on paper or the soil.

Hydromancy by water.

Icthyomancy by fishes.

Idolomancy by the use of dolls or images.

Lampadomancy by candles and lamps. Cf: Carromancy.

Lecanomancy by a basin of water.

Lithomancy by stones.

Livanomancy by the burning of frankincense.

Logarithmancy by logarithms; this method of calculation was invented by Scotsman John Napier (1550–1617) of Merchiston, Edinburgh.

Macharomancy by knives and swords.

Oinomancy by wine.

Omphilomancy by the navel.

Oniromancy by dreams.

Onomatomancy by names.

Onychomancy by the nails of fingers and toes.

Ornithomancy by birds.

Podomancy by the feet.

Psychomancy by men's souls, or by moral dispositions.

Pyromancy by fire.

Roadomancy by heavenly stars.

Sciomancy by shadows.

Spatalamancy by skin, bones and excrements.

Stareomancy by the elements.

Sternomancy by the area from the breast to the belly.

Sycomancy by figs.

Theomancy by spirit revelation.

Theriomancy by beasts.

Tuphramancy by ashes from fires; particularly popular during the feast of Beltane.

Tyromancy by the coagulation of cheese.

So witch hunters scoured the living-quarters of supposed witches for evidence of divination, and they were sure to find it; every household object had its divinatory potential.

The form of divination considered most horrific in Scotland was necromancy, which involved the inspecting and consulting of the dead. The superstitions concerning witches raiding graveyards lasted long in Scots folklore and were still alive in Robert Burn's day; he wrote in *Address To The Deil:*

> And in Kirkyards renew their leagues,
> Owre howkit dead. *exhumed*

Those who had to justify the reality of necromancy in Scotland's witch trials had as their biblical text the classic instance of necromancy in the case of the Woman of Endor who was consulted by Saul (1 Samuel 28) when he wished to destroy the Philistine army; the woman, undoubtedly a spiritualistic medium in modern thought, brought Samuel back from the dead to give advice.

It was easy for witch prosecutors to draw parallels from the primitive past. Over and above his rites for hunting, fishing, fertility and self-preservation, it is the theme of death which dominated tribal man's religion in Scotland as much as magic. To appease the spirits of the dead, to ensure for them a peaceful afterlife, to protect one's self from them, to propitiate them—these were the prime concerns of Scots tribesmen and women and the race legacy was passed on to Scotland's medieval witches.

The Scottish Witches' Gardens

All nations have their omens drear,
Their legends wild of woe and fear;
To Cambria look—the peasant see
Bethink him of Glendowery,
And shun the Spirit's blasted tree.
Marmion Sir Walter Scott

From Glenelg the narrow, twisting road hugs the foreshore of the Sound of Sleat across from Skye. For as long as anyone could remember there stood a tree at an awkward bend on the road by Eilanreach. When its branches became more and more of a hazard to passing traffic, the council felled it and the trunk and branches were sawn into manageable lengths of firewood. The logs were piled by the roadside with the word-of-mouth message that locals could help themselves to the fuel. Yet stacks of the wood still remain.

Why did the folk thereabout not make use of this valuable source of heat? According to the neighbourhood gossip, the tree had been a 'hanging tree' in the old days for murderers and robbers. To burn the wood, said the old folk, would bring bad luck. Some of the younger people laughed at the old superstition and filled their trailers with the wood. Before long they wished they hadn't. Their houses were filled with an evil smell every time a fire of the wood was lit and somehow with it there was an air of depression, and the smell was difficult to disperse.

A few persisted, but soon they too gave up burning the wood and returned what was left to the pile. The mystery of the strange smell and atmosphere remained, until someone remembered the old tale that long ago, decades before Dr Samuel Johnson and James Boswell visited Glenelg in 1773, a witch had been hanged on the tree. As everyone knew, a spiteful witch could turn herself into the spirit of a tree and use it for evil purposes. Thus the disruption of the houses was explained; it was the witch's revenge for felling her tree home.

Since the days of Celtic heathendom when the shamans of the tribes had their sacred groves of rheumatism-curing apple, lightning-deflecting hawthorn and lifespan-enhancing holly, there have been two trees in Scotland particularly associated with witches.

To bring elder wood into the house was to encourage the Devil to visit; Judas Iscariot was said to have hung himself on an elder tree. Like the folk of Glenelg, farm workers with a gift of firewood from the laird always discarded the elder for the housefire. Neither would they make cradles from elder, or shepherds' crooks or bickers (drinking vessels), nor beat an erring childing with an elder rod for fear of stunting growth. Why? Elders, the old witchlore stated, were the favourite trees in which witches hid themselves as spirits. Should you cut an elder, too, you would see it bleed. When you suspected someone of working magic against you, said the old folk of Forfar, lop an elder branch. If the next day you meet someone with a bandaged hand or arm, then that must be the person working a curse against you.

Thus the superstitious expected a witch to have an elder tree in the garden. Elder was once used to cure various conditions from warts and quinsies (tonsillitis) to sword wounds and mad dog bites. Elder bark boiled in water was often used for the falling sickness (epilepsy).

While juniper twigs were used to keep witches away from cow byres in the Western Isles, and ash sticks to herd cattle in Buchan for similar reasons, the rowan has pride of place in Scottish witchlore.

The rowan, or mountain ash, was long credited in Scotland with the power of deflecting witch curses, magically inflicted disease, evil fairies and the Evil Eye. In many a Scottish croft and bothy the cross beam of the chimney was made of rowan for this purpose, and on Quarter Days, when important business was afoot and men and women were hired or re-engaged on farm and estate, a twig of rowan was pinned to the house lintel, or the mantlepiece hung with crosses of rowan tied up with red thread for good luck, as the old saying averred:

> Rowan tree and red thread
> Gar the witches tyne their speed*cause/forfiet*

A necklace of rowan berries was a protection against satanic perils of all kinds. Even animals were draped with rowan berry garlands to help them drop their young. The rowan is equalled only by the birch in its ability to dilute curses and prevent abortions.

There's many a will been registered in Scotland containing a mention of the rowan to keep witches away from the dead. One such was that of David Richie (c1740–1811), the only person Sir Walter Scott held in some dread. Scott met the diminutive, deformed Ritchie in 1797 and immortalized him in his unsuccessful book *The Black Dwarf* (1816) as the character 'Elshender the Recluse of Mucklestane Moor'.

Richie was a devout misogynist, and his twisted torso and ugly, malevolent face made him a fearsome individual, a reputation he encouraged with the pretence of being able to wreak retributional magic on his detractors. He lived in a cottage at Woodhouse, Peeblesshire, and had a wide knowledge of flora and fauna, which he invested with magic powers. He was buried in Manor churchyard, Peebleshire, with a personally requested witch-defying rowan on his grave to guard his bones. Alas his skeleton was removed in 1821 (when the grave was opened to receive his sister's corpse) and was taken to the anatomy school at Glasgow.

Another tree long associated with the protection of the dead in Scotland was the yew, symbol of everlasting life. In the days of clan conflict in the Highlands many a chief took a piece of graveyard yew in his left hand to denounce all the witches of the place lest they combine to act with the clan's enemies. In the graveyard at Fortingall, Perthshire, a 3 000-year-old yew bears testimony to the tenacity of the belief that yews represented immortality.

Beech trees around the house attracted longevity, the witchlore said, and beech wood was a sure amulet against loss of memory, especially if attacked by a witch's curse. In Glen Moidart, Inverness, Jacobite sympathizers remembered this old wisdom when they planted seven beeches in unfailing memory of the Marquis of Tullibardine, Sir Thomas Sheridan, George Kelly, Col Strickland, Aeneas Macdonald, Sir John Macdonald and Col O'Sullivan—'The Seven men of Moidart'—who landed at Loch-nan-Uamh with Charles Edward Stewart from *Du Teillay* in 1745.

There was hardly a garden in medieval Scotland which did not have a patch devoted to herbs. Most folk knew that many plants yielded valuable medicinal substances, so the use of herbal remedies was widely practised. Those who studied their subject well also recognized the poisonous properties of certain plants and herbs, and it was just a short jump of imagination to give flora a whole variety of magical properties and every witch a knowledge of poisons. A witch's expertise in these matters was called 'wort cunning'.

The merging of this conversance with herbs and the preparation of magical potions in a cauldron is both symbolic and traditional in Scotland. This hollow vessel, mentioned rarely in trials but occurring in *Records of the Presbytery of Cupar* (1649), has obvious female associations and signified to those who worked magic the very Womb of Nature in which all kinds of sorcery could be conceived. To those who sought for ancient symbolism its three legs were emblematic of the triple Moon goddess, the patroness of witches.

The symbolism of the cauldron was superstitiously mingled with the four elements of life: *fire*, to heat the cauldron; *water*, to fill it; the fruits of the *earth* to prepare in it; and its pungent steam rising into the *air* and providing a medium in which clairvoyants might claim to see wavering shapes of future happenings, as Elspeth the Cupar witch averred in 1649.

In Scotland certain plants were considered indispensable for a witch's garden. In Elspeth Reoch's Trial in Orkney, 1616, it was recorded that she cured diseases with a herb called *melefour* (or yarrow); this was also a herb useful in divination and was tied to babies' cradles to avert witchcraft.

Monk's hood (or wolf's bane) produced the much sought-after poison aconite. While *henbane* was another poison said to be widely used by witches for head garlands for their dead, it was also used as a cure for toothache or insomnia. *Willow bark*, nicknamed 'witch's asprin', was used for similar purposes and for rheumatism. *Hemlock* was another common poison of witchlore as was *deadly nightshade*, both used to promote 'visions'.

Selago is a fine yellow powder comprising the spores of the club-moss, used by witches to enable them to understand the language of birds and beasts. Perhaps the Celtic shamans were the first to use it for their rituals as the history of its use was ancient before the 17th-century witch trials.

Datura was long known as the thorn-apple, and its strong narcotic properties induced a frenzied delirium which caused victims to dance themselves to oblivion. Dance was an important part of witch ritual and the drug-induced 'daunce endlange the kirkyaird' of 1590, mentioned in the

North Berwick Witch Trial by Pitcairn in *Criminal Trials*, so fascinated King James VI that he had the accused, Geillis Duncan, play the witches' dance tune on his trumpet.

St John's Wort is mentioned much in witchlore and was boiled in wine as a popular remedy against vomiting blood. According to medieval superstition the red spots on the plant make their appearance on 29 August, the day of St John the Baptist's beheading.

Herbs and flowers used for protection against sorcery included St John's Wort as well as verbena, cyclamen, pimpernel, bracken, fern, broom, maidenhair, ground ivy, fennel, garlic and agrimony. As the old verse says:

> Trefoil, Vervain, St John's Wort and Dill,
> Hinder all witches of their foul will.

Some anti-witch flora had beneficial properties too. *Angelica*, which according to the medieval herbaries bloomed on the Feast of the Apparition of St Michael on 8 May, combatted indigestion and head colds. *Cinquefoil* was a love-divination plant often hung on doorways to deflect witches and attract a suitor. *Clover* served a similar purpose, while *houseleek* (Jove's Beard) was allowed to grow on thatched roofs to protect against fires.

The blackberry bush, the Scots 'brummle', has a place in the nation's witchlore too. It was used as a food, a dye (the root), medicine (leaves) and for occult purposes as a garland (with ivy and woodbine) for protection against the Evil Eye. For the latter it was cultivated by the old Highland folk where it did not occur naturally. Canon J A MacCulloch in *The Misty Isle of Skye* points out that it was a magical plant of that island's tradition. In Skye, and elsewhere, a bramble hedge was thought to help protect a field of corn from bewitchment as discussed in the Isobel Goudie of Auldearn witch case of 1662.

Perhaps the most curious plant to be mentioned for the witch's garden was mandrake. A narcotic plant, the roots of which often grow into the shape of human limbs, it was long used as a source of juice for love philtres. The book called *Strange and Wondrous Plants*, which no self-respecting witch hunter would be without, stated that mandrake was deemed 'to grow under the gallows of hanged men—pulled from the ground the root emitted wild shrieks, and those who heard them were driven mad.' One way for Scots witches to collect mandrake, without being screeched to madness by the emerging plant, was to tie a hungry dog to the plant after the soil around the plant's roots had been loosened (with an ivory or iron tool). When a piece of food was placed just out of reach the dog would strain on the halter tied to the mandrake and thereby pull out the plant. The mandrake was often used by witches in potions to increase sexual powers, using the 'male' and 'female' roots as appropriate.

Many a witch swore by the powers of the trailing pearlwort, known to the Gaelic-speaking witches as *mothan*. The plant was carried on the person for efficacy in keeping airborne evil spirits away. It was tied to a woman's leg, below the knee, to stop witches—or fairies—from substituting a changeling while she was in labour. Like the mandrake it was also used for love charms, and many a Highland lass moistened her lips with the pearlwort to attract her intended.

In his *Witchcraft and Second Sight in the Highlands of Scotland*, J G Campbell showed how

Christian symbolism could be tied in with the superstitions of witchcraft for added potency:

> I will cull the pearlwort
> Beneath the fair sun of Sunday,
> Beneath the hand of the Virgin,
> In the name of the Trinity,
> Who willed it grow.
>
> While I shall keep the pearlwort,
> Without ill mine eye,
> Without harm my mouth,
> Without grief my heart,
> Without guile my death.

Foxgloves, 'witches' thimbles', have a name derived not from foxes but from fairies in their guise of the 'good folk'. The medicinal properties of the foxglove (a source of digitalis) were discovered by witches according to the old Scots tomes on folklore, but were brought into reputable medicine by Dr William Withering who observed a witch cure an old woman of dropsy by dosing her with foxglove tea. He purchased her recipe and discovered the important ingredient.

Called in Gaelic *Lus an Talaidh*, 'the enticing plant', purple orchis was collected by Highland witches from soft patches of heather. In *The Gaelic Names of Plants* John Cameron shows that this plant had male and female 'identities' and a ritual for its collection: 'It has two roots, one larger than the other, and it is in these that its magic power consists. The larger represents the man, the lesser a woman, whose affections are to be gained. The plant is to be pulled by the roots before sunrise, with the face directed to the South. Whichever root is used is to be immediately placed in spring water, care being taken that no part of the sun's surface is above the horizon. If it sinks, the person whose love is sought will prove the future husband or wife. If the charm is made for no one in particular, the root reduced to powder and put below the pillow causes dreams of the person to be married.'

Orris root was another plant used for divination. The root was bound with thread to make a pendulum; should it swing deasil (clockwise) an affirmative answer to a question was indicated and if widdershins (anti-clockwise) a negative.

The time of day when plants and herbs were collected was deemed important by witches, as the correct phase of the moon had to be calculated correctly lest negative influences destroy magical potency. In Scottish witchlore tradition, the waxing of the moon was the time for witches to plot magic constructive to their purpose; the moon's waning could work against a witch. Yet a waning moon could be harnessed too for destructive legerdemain against neighbours. Witches also thought it necessary to use a magical number of different herbs in a spell, three, seven or nine being the most common multiples used.

Not all witches' herbal potions were used in liquid form: some were powdered and sewn into small sachets as charms. When the Rev Ross Roy MacKeachie was locum minister in Kincardineshire in the 1890s he came across an old woman who, after he had noted certain herbs growing in her garden, showed him a recipe for such a dried herb charm. The minister jotted it down as a remedy against neuralgia and the swelling of joints: 'Pick docking, southernwood and fragrant orris root. Crush between sandstone and sew into a small purse, using emerald green silk dress of Venus; sew on a Friday in the increase of the moon and pin inside the clothing next to the skin'.

A witch took care in the layout of her garden, of which the centrepiece must be a tree other than the anti-witch variety. A note of the growing season of herbs and plants was taken too so that all worked together in magic harmony and were ready at any time of year to 'raise the power'.

Astrology was linked to witch herb lore from before the end of the 14th century. John Barbour (c1320–95), author of the narrative poem *The Brus*, mentions how astrology and necromancy (calling up the dead by magic so that they could be consulted about the future) were used by his character 'Bruce's hostess' to foretell the victory and kingship of Robert I, the Bruce. In time certain herbs, plants and trees were linked to a person's birth sign in the following manner:

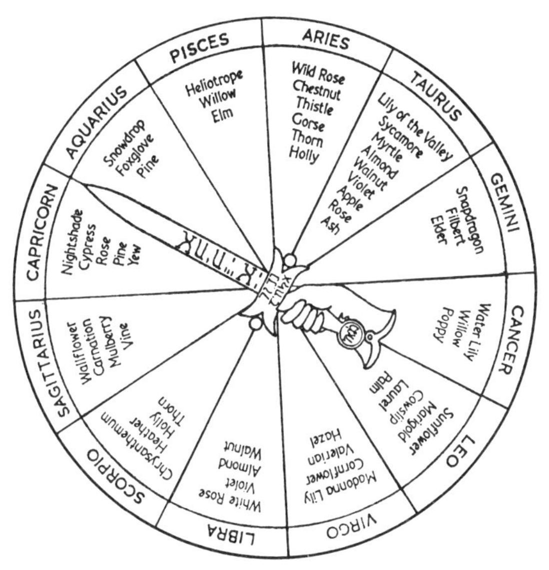

A source of running water or a well would be expected in a witch's garden. Before the Reformation wells associated with saints were very popular in Scotland, a Christianization of the sacred pools and water-cults of the early tribesmen of Scotland. Many of Scotland's so-called 'healing wells' and 'magic pools' were objects of medieval pilgrimage, particularly the more famous ones such as the now vanished well of Our Lady of Loretto, Musselburgh, and the Holy Pool of St Fillan, near Tyndrum, Perthshire. Thus as water could be used for healing it must be potent too, the old folk said, for witches to fix their curses and mix their potions.

Since the negative side of all living things could be exploited by witches, more weeds than flowers were to be expected in a witch's garden. Certain weeds were encouraged to grow by witches, say the old records, for each weed had its own occult powers.

Both witches and non-witches had their own garden alarm system. Plant parsley near your front door, the wise ones averred, so that should it begin to fade and die without reason you would know there was a witch in the neighbourhood. And no witch with an eye to his or her own safety would fail to plant a multicoloured rank of anemones near their gate, for the flowers would give warning of approaching hostile strangers.

Black Cats and Horned Toads

They ca' her witch o'Endor;
And she comes fra' Sanquhar way;
Black Bess o'the twisted lug;
'Tis her has brought us ill . . .
She's left her broomstick in the house . . .
Nor owl nor yet enchanted Bat are with unhallowed Bess . . .
The Witch of Crawick Mill Francis Merrilees

Marion Pardoun, The Witch of Hillswick, Shetland, told the court at her trial at Scalloway in 1644 that when she was going one time from Brecan to Hillswick the Devil appeared to her in the likeness of two corbies (crows). There and then he gave her the gift of being able to turn into any animal she chose. So she regularly changed herself into a 'pellack whale' (porpoise) so that she could get near to sailing vessels and upset them. But when she was bewitching cattle she preferred the guise the Devil himself chose, that of a crow. Incidentally, the belief in cattle bewitchment remained long in Shetland superstition; in the mid-1920s, the *Shetland Folk Book* notes, a certain procedure was followed by one farmer to heal a cow 'sickened through witchcraft'.

The corbie was well known in Celtic folklore as a bird of evil omen: 'Nae gude ever cam' o' killin' black crows' ran one Scots proverb. The superstition was linked in Celtic lore to 'the dark goddesses of slaughter'—the Cailleach—who, when Christianity came, turned themselves into hags or monsters to persecute mankind. A sister bird in evil omen was the raven ('corbie crow' in Scots) which helped witches achieve longevity with its powers and was the witches' representative to watch over funerals.

Another bird of witching was the yellowhammer, the 'yella yite' of Border folklore. Its erratic movements and uneven flying patterns marked it as the Devil's bird and a fit companion of witches. In the south-west of Scotland they said that the yite got its quirkiness from drinking a drop of the Devil's blood on May Day morn:

> Half a puddick, half a toad,
>   Half a yellow yorling;
> Drink a drap o'the de'ils blood,
>   On oor May Day morning.

Many have fancied that the yellowhammer's song resembles human speech and in the Mearns they identified it as the bird which gave witches warning of impending ambush. For the folk of Buchan the cry was translated thus:

> Whetil te, whetil te, whee,
> Harry my nest, an' the de'il tak ye.

Others took the strange markings on the eggs of the yellowhammer to be cabbalistic writings known only to witches.

In several parts of Scotland men and boys would sally forth on New Year's day to hunt wrens; one shot on this day ensured that the local village would be free of witchcraft for one year. In Galloway up to the 1890s wrens were caught and decorated with ribbons for protection against evil. The custom was called 'The Deckan' o'the Wren'.

In many coastal regions of Scotland the plaintive sound of the curlew was a sign of an impending storm. This bird, called a 'whaup' in Scots, was another companion of witches feared by Shetlanders who would not entertain it as a food. The word whaup was also used in Scots for a breed of goblin—a frightful sprite—which entered houses to work evil at witches' behest. The storm-petrel's appearance too foretold a storm, thus Scots seafarers called it the 'waterwitch'.

Fulmars should be left alone too as it was ill luck to meddle with them or their nests, and especially to steal their eggs. The lark the lavrock in Scots—was evilly unwholesome in Scotland as a food as well for it was a bird cursed in a special way. The devil himself had marked the bird as his own by staining three black spots under the lark's tongue; to eat the bird was to consume these three curses.

The witches of *Macbeth* used the wing of an 'owlet' for a charm of 'powerful trouble'. For many Scots, to meet an owl by daylight was unlucky as they were scouts for witches, and should they enter a house they were considered a death omen. Get on the right side of a witch, though, and she could cure you of whooping-cough by giving you owl broth. Again, a remedy for gout was to eat salted owl.

Old Scots said of the swallow that there was 'a drop o' the De'ils blood in its veins'. An old superstition told how the bird had a magic stone hidden in its body which, if taken from the swallow at the time of the Lammas full moon, could cure epilepsy and blindness. Witches wore such stones on bracelets.

It was probably from witch folklore that the farmyard rooster was believed to be a good advance guard to indicate if strangers were approaching, particularly visitors of evil intent. A cock crowing before midnight would be heard with abject terror as this indicated that a member of the household was about to die at the hands of a witch working a spell.

When you were selling up your croft or farm, the old folk said, you should never sell your hens. To do so would be to attract ill-luck and lay yourself open to witchcraft. So the hens must be given away. The death of large numbers of hens was taken as a warning that witches were about to attack the farm cattle.

Should you wake one morning and find the heart, liver and lungs of a pigeon on your doorstep, you would know that you had had a visit from someone who wanted to work evil on you. If the culprit were a witch, she would keep the rest of the pigeon to protect her own kind. Portions of a pigeon's carcass slipped into the shoe were a protection against sudden attack, said the folk of Moray. Despite being the emblem of good in many societies, the pigeon clearly had a mixed folklore in Scotland. Indeed witches would use them to mark their victims; a pigeon, or dove, flying around a person was a sure sign for the folk of Aberdeenshire's hinterland that that unfortunate was about to be bewitched to death.

In the anonymous book *A Sailor Boy's Experience* (1867), the author recounts how in the neighbourhood of Clyde shore before men went to sea they would catch a wren and pluck it. As the feathers fell they could tell if it was to be stormy at sea or if they were in danger of evil influences.

A single magpie flying away from the sun (widdershins) was considered extremely unlucky for it was out looking for specific people who were about to be bewitched. A protective measure was to spit over the right shoulder three times and once towards the direction of the magpie and say: 'Devil, Devil, I defy thee'. And, by counting the number of magpies in any group, witches were supposed to fortell events. Here is the common rhyme about magpies on the left with the witches' version underneath:

Ane for sorrow
    Ane for the person who's worked me ill
Twa for mirth
    Twa for the man I'm going to kill.
Three for a waddin'
    Three for a droonin
Fower for a birth
    Fower for a curse

Five for a fiddler
    Five for a minister's even worse,
Six for a dance
    Six for cantraips o'er the moor
Seven for Auld Scotia
    Seven for the bairnie I shall smoor
Eight for France
    Eight for the Devil I'll meet the morn.

Down the decades Scotland's witches have had their own magical helpers, as George Giffard tells us in his *Dialogue Concerning Witches* (1593):

'The witches have their spirits, some hath one, some hath more, as two, three, four, and five, some in one likeness and some in another, as like cats, weasels, toads or mice, whom they nourish with milk or a chicken, or by letting them suck now and then a drop of blood'.

The concept of a witch having a 'familiar spirit' is a key element in witch folklore of the United Kingdom in general and Scotland in particular. As was seen in the Marion Pardoun case, after a witch had made a contract with the Devil, he left behind some 'low demon' in animal form to advise her and perform small, malicious errands, including murder. 'Each of us', said Isobel Goudie the Auldearn witch, 'has a spirit to wait upon us, when we please to call upon him'.

As Giffard shows, witches at various times have been accused of having spirits in the form of animals. His list can be augmented for Scottish lore to include dogs, ferrets, rats and insects. But the animal most associated with witches is the cat. This beast has probably the longest folkloric history of all animals, from its veneration in Ancient Egypt as the god of Pasht.

Cats have a wide range of superstitions associated with them. It is very bad luck (say actors) to kick a cat, and unlucky too for one to be found on board a ship. Some said that cats could raise storms. In his book *Sentimental Tommy* (1896), Sir James Matthew Barrie, remembering the old Kirriemuir superstition, wrote that Ballingall's cat washed its face in 'a deliberate attempt to bring on rain'.

The very name 'cat' was a taboo word amongst Aberdeenshire fishermen, for instance, because of the witch associations. In *Criminal Trials* (1590), Robert Pitcairn noted how in the Agnes Sampson of Prestonpans witch case the accused had 'baptized a cat' by passing it through 'the links of a cruick [crook]' and 'thryis under the chimney' and had thrown the cat into the sea to make boats perish.

As late as 1718 William Montgomery of Caithness testified that he was nightly harassed by hordes of witch-induced cats prowling around his house and 'talking in human language'. Yet Robert Kerse of Dalkeith, who was 'tormented with witchcraft and disease', had the curse of witchcraft raised from him when the Wise Woman of Dalkeith transferred the curse into a cat.

It was a common idea that if a witch, when in the form of an animal, received a wound, she would still bear the wound in the same place on regaining human shape. Such a case was researched by one young medical practitioner for his patron Sir Walter Scott. In his youth Dr Wilkie of Bowden, near Eildon Hill in the Borders, collected folktales for Sir Walter and brought to light the 'Littledean Case'. Littledean Tower was an ancient baronial house in Roxburghshire some one and a half miles north-east of Maxton village. This was how Dr Wilkie's journal described the case:

'The laird [Harry Gilles] of Littledean was

extremely fond of hunting. One day, as his dogs were chasing a hare, they suddenly stopped, and gave up the pursuit, which enraged him so much that he swore the animal they had been hunting must be one of the Witches of Maxton. No sooner had he uttered the word [witch] than hares appeared all round him, so close that they even sprang over the saddle before his eyes, but still none of his hounds would give them chase. In a fit of anger, [the laird] jumped off his horse and killed the dogs on the spot, all but one large black hound, who at that moment turned to pursue the largest hare. Remounting his horse, he followed the chase, and saw the black hound turn the hare and drive it directly towards him. The hare made a spring as if to clear his horse's neck, but the laird dexterously caught hold of one of the forepaws, drew out his hunting knife, and cut it off; after which the hares, which had been so numerous, also disappeared. Next morning Laird Harry heard that a woman of Maxton had lost her arm in some unaccountable manner; so he went straight to her house, pulled out the hare's foot (which had changed in his pocket to a woman's hand and arm), and applied it to the stump. It fitted exactly. She confessed her crime, and was drowned for witchcraft the same day in the well by the young men of Maxton.'

This story, and many others, bears testimony to the fact that in local Scottish cognizance the hare was the most popular animal for a witch to turn herself into. Again Robert Pitcairn cites the Isobel Goudie case and tells how skilled she was in transmogrification into a hare. She and her fellow witches recited this rhyme as part of their 'turning' spell:

> I shall go intill ane hare,
> With sorrow an' sych an' meikle care;
> And I shall go in the Devil's name
> Ay while I come here again.

And when they had worked their magic in the hare's form Scots witches would recite this to emerge as human again:

Hare, hare, God send thee care;
I am in a hare's likeness now;
But I shall be a woman even now,
Hare, hare, God send thee care.

The rather unattractive aspect of the toad made it an obvious creature to associate with witches both as a familiar to help with witchcraft and as a disguise. The witches of *Macbeth* had good reason to add a toad to their brew:

Toad, that under coldest stone,
Days and nights has thirty-one
Sweltered venom sleeping got,
Boil thou first i'the charmed pot.

Witches and all workers of folk medicine knew that this reptile exudes the poison bufotenine and bufagin from its skin glands if it is roughly seized. But the witches of Scotland were after a much more powerful tool when they went toad hunting. The toad jewel or toadstone was a powerful magic charm as the working of the legendary Toadstone of the Mearns bore testimony. With it whole communities were cured.

Amongst historians of Scottish witchcraft the toadstone was called *crapaudina* and its magic powers had been known since the 13th century in Scotland from the Latin works of Albertus Magnus. But it was Thomas Lupton, in his *Book of Notable Things* (1660), who told scholars how the toadstone might be authenticated. 'You shall knowe', averred Lupton, 'whether the tode-stone be the right and perfect stone or not. Holde the stone before a tode, so that he may see it; and, if it be right and true stone, the tode will leape towarde it, and make as though he would snatch it. He envieth so much that man should have that stone.'

The 'stone', in reality a bone from the head of the common toad, was most efficacious, the magic-workers said, as an antidote to any poison. Some who espoused witchcraft wore the stone in finger rings or on bracelets. The one kept in the Mearns was a recognized amulet against plague.

Because Scotland was largely an agricultural, cattle-raising community in historical times, these beasts repeatedly appear in witch lore as victims of bewitchment. Thefts of cattle by witches were regularly reported and Scottish witches were deemed able to steal milk by creating a kind of ectoplasmic magic milking tube.

Writing in 1895, R C Maclagen told the story of how a farmer of Bernera, near Glenelg, west Invernesshire, suspected that his cows gave so little milk because they were bewitched. He plaited a rope of horsehair with rowan twigs and haltered one of the beasts with it. The cow when released made its way to a certain woman's cottage where it tossed its head and bellowed in her direction. The local folk accepted this as a clear indication of her guilt and she was driven out of the area.

Some cattle were so far gone in their bewitchment that they remained 'witch kine' or 'fairy livestock', which could only be shot with a silver arrow. Certain areas of Scotland were associated with these cattle, which were deemed to dwell in lochs after their final enchantment. Loch Rannoch and Loch Awe were cited as places where they dwelt and James Hogg, bynamed the Ettrick Shepherd, wrote this of the 'witch water cow' of St Mary's Loch in Yarrow: 'A farmer in the neighbourhood got a breed of her that multiplied and throve well until the farmer somehow outraged or offended her; whereupon one fine night the old dam came out of the loch and gave such a roar that the surrounding hills shook again, upon which her progeny, nineteen in number, followed her quietly into the water and were never seen again.'

As late in folklore history as 1884 a witch water cow was rumoured to have been seen in a loch in the parish of Gairloch, Ross-shire.

Professor George Sinclair in *Satan's Invisible World Discovered* (1871) talks of one Beattie Long of Pittenweem, Fife, who had the power to make horses fly. Indeed in Celtic belief a spirit horse—a minion of Epona, Celtic goddess of horses—conveyed the departed to the Realm of the Dead, so it was understandable that the supposed occult powers of the horse should be transferred to witchcraft.

Celts also buried horse bones in the foundations of their dwellings to protect inmates from evil spirits, and many a Celtic settlement had a horse's skull above the main gateway for similar purposes. From the days of the Celts horses were deemed to have the second sight; a famous legend recalls how St Columba's horse foresaw its master's death and 'shed bitter tears', so horse bones were a required part of witches' paraphernalia.

A Scottish witch seeking to gallop to her sabbat meeting might borrow a horse without permission, returning the sweating beast to its stable by morning. Many a stable had a flint with a hole in it hung above the entrace to protect the horses therein from being 'hagge-ridden'. In Caithness and Sutherland they believed that another mode of witch travel was to enchant a human with a 'magic bridle' and ride them during sleep.

The 'Wild Horse' riding over Scottish hills and moors in a mad chase pursued by witches is a common enough theme in Scots folklore verse, and Robert Burns used a memory of it in his *Tam o'Shanter:*

> So Maggie runs, the witches follow,
> Wi' monie an eldritch skriech and hollow.

Go to a witch, said the old folk, and she'll cure

you of deafness by mixing ants' eggs with onion juice; by dropping a little into the affected ear hearing would be restored. Likewise a live spider in a pat of butter would cure jaundice, but the beetle had a more sinister association with witches. In *The Key to the Forth* (1858), John Jack tells how the beetle was feared in St Monans, Fife, where it was called a 'goloch'. Old St Monans folk held the beetle to be a familiar of witches and cited the case of the local witch Grizzie who had brought many a bad spell of weather to the locality and may a bereavement to fishing families through conjuring with beetles.

As a part of bewitchment it was important, the wise ones averred, for a witch to obtain control over the souls of her enemies. She sometimes did so with the use of mice. It is an old Scottish superstition that mice came to embody the souls of those who dwelt in the house they infested, so should a witch wish to have influence over a household she would endeavour to trap a mouse from the dwelling. In some areas of Scotland this belief was associated instead with rats, whose heads were so potent for use in witchcraft curses that cats would not eat them.

In Morayshire it was said that pigs could 'see the wind' and they were included in weather-lore proverbs; a tempest would be impending if a pig rushed around with a straw in its mouth. Thus local seamen thought them ominous beasts. To avert a storm brewed up by a witch riding a black pig, the Moray fishermen would mutter 'cauld iron', the metal being a well-known deflector of witchcraft.

Scotland developed its own folkloric fauna and one fabulous beast was shared by Elfhame—the realm of the fairies—and by the witches. The water-kelpie is a creature that was deemed to live in deep pools of rivers and streams. It was never a familiar of witches but they long tried to discover its secrets.

The water-kelpie usually took the form of a black horse and was generally nocturnal in its habits. For many who were induced to ride the

water-kelpie, after staying overlong at the local inn, it spelled death; for the beast would gallop off to its lair beneath the water with the victim clinging to its mane. Because pools were their habitat, some of Scotland's famous rivers have been cited as more dangerous than others. Hence the Border folkrhyme:

> Tweed said to Till, what gars ye rin so still?
> *makes you run*
> Till said to Tweed, though ye rin wi' speed,
> An' I rin slaw.
> For ae man that ye droon,
> I droon twa.

Witches endeavoured to capture water-kelpies because they were the best of all work horses, never tiring at the gallop, and never flagging between the shafts. Yet the beasts could be a nuisance if not kept on a tight rein. One Peeblesshire story told how a water-kelpie, which slipped from its witch mistress's bridle, began to terrorize a blacksmith and his family.

Things got so bad that the blacksmith resolved to kill the water-kelpie. But how? A witch from Innerleithen advised him that this could only be done with iron. The local story told how 'the smith prepared two long, sharp-pointed spits of iron and repaired to his home. He put a large fire on the hearth and laid the two spits upon it. In a short time the water-kelpie made his usual disruptive appearance. The smith waited his opportunity;

and with all his might drove the red-hot spits into the creature's sides. Instantly the water-kelpie fell to a pile of ashes.'

Yet despite all the dangers, witch and non-witch alike thought it worth the risk to dabble with water-kelpies, for where these beasts were to be found so were heaps of lost treasure.

Witches said that mole pelt was good to repair the skin of the chest ripped open by sword or battleaxe, and that of the 'thraw mouse' (fieldmouse) would prevent paralysis of the feet, but for good favours a sheep should be raised in a house's glebe. Scotland is perhaps unique in having the sheep mentioned as one of the familiars of witches. A witch was endeavouring to cast bad luck on a farm when the sheep gave birth to an unusually large amount of non-white sheep; this old superstition was mirrored in the children's rhyme:

> Baa, sheep, baa, how many lambs have you today?
> A black and a grey, a red and a bay,
> They have not been counted for many a day.

The records of the Presbytery of Kelso for 1660 note an admonition of one John Brown, a weaver, for calling his neighbour a name that struck terror into Scottish folk: 'werewolf'. Scots witches were deemed to have the power lycanthropy, the ability to change themselves into wolves. 'Were' is the Old English word for 'man'; thus a werewolf was half-man/witch, half wolf.

Undoubtedly the memory of Scotland's wolf packs, in the minds of rural folk in particular, stemmed from a tribal worship of the wolf, possibly given cult status by the Norse raiders with their mythology of Fenris the Wolf, the troublemaker of the Scandinavian Heaven. Places in Scotland containing the Gaelic word *loarn* (wolf), like Lorn in Argyll, by Loch Leven and Loch Awe, might be a relic of a local wolf cult. Nevertheless, by medieval times the folklore of the wolf had tied itself to an acknowledgement of the *beast in man*.

Wolves probably died out in the Scottish Lowlands by the 13th century, but there were still wolves in the Highlands in the 18th century; tradition says the last wolf was slain in 1650 by Sir Ewen Cameron of Lochiel. So the rarity of the wolf as witch mania spread in Scotland made it a mysterious beast, naturally linked with witchcraft.

The belief that witches could turn themselves into wolves was given credence by King James VI and I in his *Daemonologie*. Potions of belladonna and datura were made to facilitate this transformation. A witch/werewolf could only be killed with a dagger or bullet of metal of the Moon (silver).

Cures, Curses and Charms

Hemlock, juice of aconite
With poplar leaves and roots bind tight.
Mix watercress and oil
To rabbit's fat and boil.
Some bat's blood and belladonna too
Will cure the agues that misuse you.
Mary Stuart's Herbal

Patrick Adamson, who held the title of Archbishop of St Andrews from 1575 until his death in 1592, was at the end of his tether with the established medical practitioners of his day. Try as they might they were unable to cure him of his many ills. Instead he turned to the witch 'Phetanissa' for relief. The traditional story *The Legend of Adamsoune* does not say if His Grace was cured. It does note, though, that the witch used 'heather . . . cut off at new moon . . . and forty weeds'.

The papers of the great witch trials of Scotland are full of lists of cures that witches were said to have used for a wide range of ailments. In 1629, for instance, the witch Isobel Young of East Barnes, East Lothian, used salt she had panned herself to cure skin conditions. And Isobel Thompson, nicknamed 'Premack', of Moray made a cure for broken limbs with a plaster of 'swine's sawine [blood], rassat [a herb], wax, black pepper, honey and cannell [coal]'.

Trial transcripts show that witches in Scotland were reckoned to have three ways of effecting cures on what ailed humanity: transference, association and sacrifice.

'Transference' forced an illness out of the afflicted and into something else, usually an inanimate object like a stone or a tree. In the book *Witches of Renfrewshire* (1877) we have the story of John Dougall, under the date 1695, who was accused of a distinctive type of transference magic. He is said to have endeavoured to relieve convulsions in a neighbour by forcing them into parings and clippings from the man's own nails and hair 'from his eyebrows and the crown of his head' all 'bound up in a clout [rag] with a halfpence'.

The use of coins in cures was well established in 16th and 17th-century Scotland and was associated with the Cult of Chiefs. Monarchs were thought to have the 'healing touch', particularly for the 'King's Evil' (scrofula). In the chapel of Glamis Castle in 1716 the Old Pretender—King James III and VIII to the Jacobites—'touched' those so afflicted and gave them a gold coin as a 'sealing agent' for the cure.

In 'association' witches worked a cure that stopped a disease in its tracks. As the old rhyme said:

> As this bean-shell rots away
> So your wart shall soon decay.

Sometimes a witch would 'sacrifice' a small animal like a vole or a bird like a sparrow to remove illness from someone who consulted her. But more often than not the 'sacrifice' cure involved plants. For example, the *History of the Province of Moray* (1827) tells us how a local witch passed children with 'hectic fever', or consumption, three times through a wreath of woodbine 'cut during the increase of March moon'.

In Orkney they believed that illness was caused by a 'malevolent worm' that had to be rooted out; the best way to remove it was to bathe the afflicted in 'Forespoken Water' from particular burns and wells. In Hoy the water was used as a general cure for all witchcraft:

> In the name of Him that can cure and kill,
> This water shall cure all earthly ill,
> Shall cure the blood and flesh and bone,
> For ilka one there is a stone;
> May [he or she] flee all trouble, sickness, pain,
> Cure without and cure within,
> Cure the heart, and horn and skin.

The Hereditary Curers were still active in the Scottish Highlands in the 1930s. Donald Mackenzie, the folklorist, found some practising their ancient skills in the Western Islands. Two centuries earlier they would have been burned for witchcraft, but in the glens where no medical practitioner ever went their craft had survived.

Another group of folk-healers which ran the risk of being accused of witchcraft was the 'charmers'. Again these folk were from family groups thought to inherit skills, but certain families seemed to specialize in certain cures; one family might cure eye diseases and another skin ailments. Others were called 'blood stoppers' as they seemed to be able to staunch the flow of blood from wounds.

These 'skeelies', 'canny folk', or 'charmers with the gift' were obviously skilled in using faith, suggestion and perhaps mesmerism. But those who were unsuccessful or pretended to work cures left themselves open to charges of witchcraft. Witness this case from the *Presbytery Book of Strathbogie* (1843):

'Apryl 12, 1637, Issobel Malcolme, parishioner of Botarye, summoned to this daye for charming, compeared, and confessed that she had beene in vse of charmeing this twenty years, and being requyred to name some of these whome she had charmed, she named Jeane Rudderfuird, spouse to James Gordoune, in Torrisoyle, and [Mistress] Innes, spouse to John Ogilvye, of Miltoune; she confessed that she had charmed both these gentlewomen for the bairne bed; and sicklyke, she confessed that she had charmed ane chyldes sore eye in Bade, within the parish of Ruven.'

Issobel Malcolme was lucky; she got away with a caution from the Presbytery Moderator, Robert Jameson, who said time may prove her 'yet more guiltye'.

A glance through the documents associated with witch trials brings to light a number of traditional 'witch cures' for various ailments:

HEADACHE: House-leek (which was encouraged to grow on the thatch of cottages) should be pounded and made into a head poultice.

EVIL EYE: 'Go to a ford, where the dead and the living cross, draw water from it, pour it into a coggie [a wooden vessel for holding milk, ale and so on] with three girds [rings] over a crosset shilling [a medieval coin], and then sprinkle the water over the victim of the ill ee . . . ' Some added that the Trinity should be invoked as a rider.
HICCUPS: Repeat this:

> My love's ane
> The hiccups twa;
> When my love likes me,
> The hiccups awa.

SPRAIN: In Shetland they used this recitation cure:

> Our Saviour rade
> His forefoot slade
> Our Saviour lichtit down.
> Sinew to sinew, vein to vein.
> Joint to joint, and bane to bane,
> Mend thou in God's name.

The incantation took place after the affected limb was bound with a linen thread tied with nine knots.
ASTHMA: Drink wild carrot juice.
BRUISES: Solomon's seal root ground on to a bread poultice.
RASHES: Rub with juice of primrose.
BURNS: Blow three times on the burn and bathe with balm.

In the history of witchcraft in Scotland these folk-medicine cures went through three stages of development. Most of them stemmed from the nature cures of the primitive tribes which were given more sinister 'witch' overtones when witch mania prevailed. But when the craze died out the cures reverted to folk-medicine again, with the recipes for the 'cures' taking a more folksy tone, their evil overtones subdued by the use of rhyme. For example, a cure for sleeplessness using camomile flowers, once to be found in witchlore, was later rendered thus:

If they be laid under man's head,
He shall sleep as if he were dead.
He shall never dream or waken,
Till from under his head it be taken.

And the witches' cure for nettle stings, the application of dock leaves, was woven into a children's nursery couplet:

In dock, out nettle,
Don't let the blood settle.

In the rural society that was old Scotland, in which people believed that there was a physical set of places called Heaven and Hell, and that white (good) and black (bad) magic actually existed, it is not surprising that the power of the curse was accepted. The supposed power of cursing was therefore seen to actually work by those cursed falling into a decline and depression brought on by their belief.

Cursing had its origins in tribal Scotland where shamans ritually denounced the evil spirits deemed to thwart daily life. This was recalled as a race memory by succeeding generations who coupled the superstition with the apparently mysterious stone monuments left by these forebears. Thus standing stones and cursing lore were united.

All over Scotland on hills and in fields are single stones and groups that the good folk pointed out as cursing stones used by witches. For instance at Cromarty there is the boulder known in Gaelic as *Clach na Mallachd* ('Stone of Cursing'). Upon this stone witches stood or knelt to do their maledictions as witnessed in the story of Kennedy of Leanach in Lochaber which recites:

She sprang . . . on a grey stone
Of the field to pronounce his doom.

From stones like these witches could control the wind and rain as they stood gesticulating, faces white with ecstatic emotion.

Others said that the stones contained spirits that could be released; a superstition common amongst the Gaels, with their stones—*coach anama*—containing spirits of heroes of their mythology. In some parts of Scotland folk would tap the stones in a ritualistic way to try and release the spirits. In the case of the Auldearn witches of 1662 there is the testimony that one witch recited this as she tapped on a monolith with a rag-wrapped stone:

> I knock this rag upon this stone,
> To raise the wind in the devil's name,
> It shall not lie until I please again.

Some witches would sell curses in the form of incantations or potions. As late as 1814 a woman called Bessie Millie of Stromness, Orkney, sold curses to thwart enemies. She also vended 'winds by the Devil's help to seamen'; Sir Walter Scott bought one and noted it in his diary.

The cursing of a family through 'several generations' is a common theme in Scottish witch, ghost and fairy stories. In his biography of his famous father-in-law Sir Walter Scott, John Gibson Lockhart tells of the Laidlaws who were cursed by a witch: ' . . . the Laidlaws who were rich and prosperous, and held rank among the best gentry in Tweeddale; . . . in some evil hour [an ancestress of the Laidlaw's was accused of witchcraft by her husband] . . . she, in her anger, cursed the name and lineage of Laidlaw. Her youngest son, who stood by, implored her to revoke the malediction; but in vain. Next day, however, on the renewal of his entreaties, she carried him with her into the woods, made him slay a heifer, sacrificed it to the power of evil in his presence and then, collecting the ashes in her apron, invited the youth to see her commit them to the river. "Follow them", she said, "from stream to pool, as long as they float visible, and as many streams as you shall then have passed, for so many generations shall your descendants prosper. After that, they shall, like the rest of the name, be poor, and take their part in my curse." The streams he counted were nine.' William Laidlaw of the ninth generation lost all.

Another few facets of witch curses were woven into Gallovidian legend and used by Scott in his book *The Bride of Lammermoor* (1819). The story concerned the daughter of James Dalrymple, Viscount Stair, who as Lord President and Privy Councillor was a man of great influence but despised by his neighbours. Janet Dalrymple married Laird Baldoon on 12 August 1699 after apparently jilting Lord Rutherford. Local legend wove four explanations for the sudden death of Janet soon after her marriage.

Some said that Janet married against her mother's will and was cursed to death by her mother who bewitched Laird Baldoon to undertake the final blow. Others averred that Lady Stair had forced her daughter to marry Baldoon despite her engagement to Rutherford and that Janet had died raving after attacking her husband. Yet more said that Rutherford attached Baldoon and Janet died of fright, while the rest claimed that Janet had called upon the Devil to carry her off because she had jilted Rutherford. Behind it all, most agreed, was the witch who had gained status as Lady Stair. Local lampoons, quoted in sources such as *A*

Second Book of Scottish Pasquils (1828), identified Lady Stair as 'a daughter of Belzebub':

> Whose malice oft wes wreckit at home,
> On the curst cubs of her owne womb.

Sir Walter Scott, in fact, collected Scottish witch curses and used them in his works. Some time after he became Sheriff of Selkirkshire in 1799, Scott heard a case concerning a supposed Selkirk witch who was so successful in rearing chickens that she was thought to have prospered through nefarious means. In the poverty-stricken early 1800s she was finding it difficult to obtain grain for her birds and asked a local farmer for 'a peck of oats'. He refused, whereupon she cursed him with the prognostication that he would never propser. On his way to Dalkeith market soon afterwards a wheel fell off his wagon and sacks of his grain fell into a burn.

The farmer denounced her as a witch to Scott, who pointed out that the laws against witchcraft had by then been repealed. Scott dismissed the case with a caution to the woman not to make threatening statements. She replied, miffed: 'I ken na how it is. But something aye comes after my words when I am ill-guided. . . ' Scott remembered the case and made a cameo of it in the dialogue of *The Heart of Midlothian* (1818), mixing in Border superstition about witch curses. The character Davie Deans says of the witch figure Ailie MacClure that she 'practises her abominations, spaeing folks' fortunes wi' egg-shells, and mutton-bones, and dreams and divinations, whilk is a scandal to ony Christian land to suffer sic a wretch to live. . . '

Witches were thought to deal in charms, amulets and talismans. A charm could be a spell, a form of words or an occult object, whereas an amulet was a charm object to deflect evil and a talisman a charm object to induce magic powers.

Janet White of Selkirkshire was a skilled 'verbal' charmer and was 'admonished in the presence of the congregation' at the Kirk o' the Forest by the

Presbytery for attempts to thus cure a child. And the *Register of the Presbytery of Lanark* (1623–1709) cites Bessie Smith of Lesmahago as one who could invoke cures by spoken charms of 'buick and beil' [book and bell].

Pins, coins, red string, holy water, horse shoes, human and animal spit, amber beads and bags of salt were all used as charms, amulets and talismans in Scottish witchcraft practice. In *The Exchequer Rolls of Scotland* we find a royal use for an amulet called the 'chemise of St Margaret'. Queen Margaret who died in 1093 was the Hungarian-born wife of Malcolm Canmore, King of Scots. After a pious life she was buried in all her sanctity at Dunfermline Abbey which she had founded around the date of her marriage to Malcolm III, 1069, as a church dedicated to the Holy Trinity. That church developed into the great Abbey of Dunfermline and at the Reformation the bones of Queen Margaret (she was canonized in 1260 as St Margaret of Scotland) were spirited away by the faithful along with a portion of other relics including a gown (dubbed a 'chemise'—*camisam beate Margarete regine)* she had worn. This relic was used as amuletic swaddling clothes against bewitchment at the birth of James III (1452, St Andrews) and James V (1512, Linlithgow).

More bizarre charms included churchyard mould—soil taken from the grave of a newly buried corpse—which John Reid says in *Art Rambles in Shetland* (1896) was used as an amulet against tuberculosis. 'Water taken from the tops of Three Waves' was equally potent.

The entry for 10 September 1640 in *The Presbyterie Book of Kirkcaldie* (1630–53) tells how the supposed witch Margaret Lindsay was 'compeared' for 'spitting in a bairnes face of the fallen sickness', and John R Tudor averred in *Orkneys and Shetlands* (1833) that in those islands dog-spittle was used as a charm for animals unable to swallow. Others relied on holy water as a more sanitary charm, particularly the healing waters of Loch Morar sealed in a vial.

The book *Carnock: Ancient and Modern Village*

Life (1895) gives an intriguing charm to deflect witchcraft using numbers. A magic square was written thus:

5	10	3
4	6	8
9	2	7

Whichever way the number were added the result would be 18, a number that was sure to deflect evil spirits in the lore of this West Fife village.

Many of Scotland's prominent and famous families had charms which were handed down as heirlooms after being acquired by an ancestor from those who could fill them with magic potential. Here is a selection of those considered good agents against witchcraft, remembering of course that they were deemed dangerous in the hands of witches whose powers would be enhanced.

The Maclean of Duart *Leug* (jewel) is a ridged stone with a silver mount; the charm came from Ross of Mull. It is as powerful as the *Clach Bhuai* a rock crystal in an eight-sided, pearl-studded silver disc—the Glenorchy Charm Stone of the Campbell earls of Breadalbane and Holland. The silver-mounted rich crystal charm stones of the Mackenzies of Ardloch were used as regularly it seems as the *Clach-Dearg* (Stone of Ardvorlich) of the Stewarts of Ardvorlich. One of the most distinctive charm stones is the Keppoch Royal Crystal, affixed by a bird's claw to a silver chain, which belongs to the Macdonnels of Keppoch. This charm was dipped in water to make a magic cordial:

> Let me dip thee in the water,
> Thou yellow, beautiful gem of power!
> In water of purest wave . . .
> In the name of the Apostles twelve,
> In the name of Mary, virgin of virtues,
> And in the name of the Holy Trinity

And all the shining angels.
A blessing on the gem,
A blessing on the water,
And a healing of all bodily ailments
To each suffering creature.

Other charms also made up elixirs, for example the Lockerbie Penny. 'It is put in a cleft stick, wrote the folklorist William Henderson (1879), 'and a well is stirred round with it, after which the water is bottled off and given to any animal so affected [ie, by madness].'

The Black Penny of Humebyers, Berwickshire, was potent against insanity too, as was 'Burbeck's Bone' belonging to the Campbells of Burbeck. This charm was so useful that it made a regular income for its owners by being rented out.

The Willox family, though, the landowners of north-east Scotland, did not let their 'Witch Ball and Bridle' out of their hands. This was a glass ball and a brass hook said to have been cut from a kelpie's bridle when it was caught trying to disappear into Loch Ness.

Some charms were collected because of their historic associations. No one could assail the Clan Donnachaidh (Robertsons) while they retained the *Clach-na-Bratach* (Stone of the Standard) said to have been picked up in the field of Bannockburn (1314).

The provenance of some charms is well attested in wills and testaments. In the *Memorials of the Family of Wemyss* (1888) we have this note: 'Charm left in the will of Anna Balfour, Lady Elcho, dated 1649; bequeathed the "bloodstane braislett" [bloodstone bracelet] with "Doctor Arnot's Stone" and "teid ston ring" [toadstone].' The bloodstone—a green chalcedony, with blood-like spots of red jasper—was considered in Scotland to be the most powerful spell-breaking charm, and many a witch believed that at certain times the stone glowed red and within its fire future events could be seen. Others used bloodstones to discover witches; it if grew hot to the touch a witch was near, and if it was pointed at a suspected witch it would make her confess.

Besides curing, cursing and charming, the witches of Scotland carried out ritual charm-making for two important magic functions: transvection and invisibility.

Everyone knew that a witch was able to fly, and Scots children were taught to break a hole in the bottom of the shell of their breakfast egg to ensure that a witch could not use it as a sky boat. The most common flying tool associated with witches was a twig besom (sweeping brush) but any stick, pole, or shovel would do for the practised witch to dive and weave across the chimneys and hills. These were the vehicles, how did a witch get them aloft?

There's many a recipe for transvection quoted in Scots witches' potion books and several include the deadly plant aconite. In reality, a dose of an aconite-based nostrum, if it did not kill you, would probably give the hallucination of flight. A safer way was to use the Devil's Brushes, the common fern which is found all over Scotland. In past days it was associated with thunder and lightning and helped protect a house from storm disasters. To help with transvection, by harnessing the powers of wind and rain and thunderbolts, witches would place a few seeds of fern in a purse to hang at the girdle.

Ferns were also the base for an ointment which, when spread on the hands, allowed a witch to launch herself into the sky as a swimmer dives. Once aloft, the fern would render the witch invisible.

In Scotland the use of amulets, talismans and faith-healing charms was a capital offence. To make sure all inquisitors understood the position lawyers such as Sir George Mackenzie made the point clear. This is from Mackenzie's *Laws and Customs of Scotland* (1678): 'Though charms be not able to produce the effects that are punishable in witches, yet since these effects cannot be produced without the Devil, and [since] he will not employ himself at the desire of any who have not resigned themselves wholly to him, it is very just that the users of these should be punished, being guilty at least of apostasy and heresy.'

The superstitious, whose days and hours were governed by portents from weather, chance and the activities of birds and animals, could lay by them counter-charms against witchcraft. Several Scots folk used religious tokens retained after the Reformation and others recited prayers. Those who remembered the medieval Church might add a Latin prayer or two or a repetition of *in nomine patris et filii et spiritus sancti* ('in the name of the

Father and of the Son and of the Holy Spirit') in the privacy of their own chambers.

But many more trusted only in the three most potent anti-witch charm devices—a piece of iron (a nail or piece of wire), a length of red wool, and a sliver of mountain ash; all of these were cited as potent in the trial of Janet Leisk of Aberdeen in 1597. Her powers of persuasion—which the superstitious said were more potent with her skills of charm-making—were obviously successful because she was found not guilty.

A Witch Gazetteer

When the grey owl has three times hooed,
When the grimy cat has three times mewed,
When the tod has yowled three times i'the wud

fox/wood

At the reid mune cowrin' ahint the clud,

red moon crouching behind the cloud

When the stars has cruppen deep ' the drift

crept

Lest cantrips pyke them oot o' the lift

witches' spells steal them out of the sky

Up horses a', but mair adowe!
Ride, ride to Lochar-brig-knowe!

Memoirs of Nithsdale and Galloway Song
Robert Harley Cromek (1770–1812)

Many hills, stone circles, menhirs, craigs and woods in Scotland have acquired the prefix 'Witch' over the centuries. Some of them were genuinely associated with historic witch mania, superstitious customs or local rites, while others just possessed a spooky aspect. Here are a few which still live in folk memory of the days when witches were accepted as a reality.

A

ABERTYNE Tayside
Here was to be found a pool for ducking witches. Suspects were subject to the ordeal to determine guilt; if the witch did not drown she was guilty, if she drowned she was deemed innocent.

APPLECROSS Ross and Cromarty
Here lived the witch of Loch Carron skilled at healing sick children by wrapping charms in their clothing. People would come from miles around to seek her help.

AUCHENCROW Berwickshire
This Borders village was famous for its 'Edencraw Witches', a title based on the local pronunciation of the village name. The last of these witches, Margaret Girvin, died around 1806. Sir Alexander Hume of Reston, as Sheriff, had seven witches burned 'before the Revolution' at the coastal village of Coldingham. In 1700 Thomas Cook of Chirnside was indicted for 'scoring' a witch from Auchencrow. 'Scoring' meant that a suspected witch was scratched under the nose to draw blood, and thereby break her power to cast spells. The large number of anti-witch elderberry hedges in the neighbourhood of Auchencrow was attributed to the witches' presence.

AUCHTERGAVEN Tayside
At Meikle Obney is the Witch's Stone, which legend says was dropped from the apron of a witch as she flew across the county to Perth.

AULDEARN Nairn
The site of the famous Isobel Goudie witch trial of 1662, whose case inspired cartoonists like George Cruickshank to lampoon the popular witch superstitions. The prehistoric stone circle of Auldearn is pointed out as the place where Isobel Goudie's coven met, and the old kirk was where she was baptized a witch.

B

BALMORAL Kincardine and Deeside
Queen Victoria made her first visit to Scotland in 1842 and the Balmoral estate was bought by the Royal Family in 1852. The queen maintained a great interest in the supernatural and encouraged the ancient local rite of 'burning the witch' at Hallowe'en. Alexander Macdonald recounted the custom in *Scottish Notes and Queries:*

'A huge bonfire was kindled in front of [Balmoral] Castle, opposite the main doorway. The Clansmen were mustered, arrayed in highland garb. At a signal, headed by a band, they marched toward the palace. The bonfire was kindled so as to be in full blaze when the procession reached it. The interest of the promenade was centred on a trolley on which there sat the effigy of a hideous old woman or witch called the Shandy Dann. Beside her crouched one of the party holding her erect while the march went forward to the bagpipes' strain. As the building came in sight, the pace was quickened to a run, then a sudden halt was made a dozen yards or so from the blaze. Here, amid breathless silence, an indictment is made why this witch should be burned to ashes, and with no one to appear on her behalf – only this *advocatus diaboli,* paper in hand – she is condemned to the flames. With a rush and a shout and the skirling of bagpipes, the sledge and its occupants are hurled topsy-turvy into the fire, whilst the mountaineer springs from the car at the latest safe instant. There follow cheers and hoots of derisive laughter, as the inflammable wrappings of the Shandy Dann crackle and splutter out.

'All the while the residents at the castle stand enjoying this curious rite, and no one there entered more heartily into it than the head of the Empire herself.'

BANCHORY Kincardine and Deeside

The area was once famous for the prophecies and occult assistance given to all comers by the famous 'Witches of Strathbogie'. One case is written up in local history and was set in the days of Mary, Queen of Scots.

In 1562 the queen led her army against the 5th Earl of Huntly. As chief of the Gordons, the earl commanded much allegiance in the area and had direct access to the soothsaying women of Strathbogie. Before the battle with Mary's army the earl was told by the witches that 'After the battle you'll lie in the Tolbooth of Aberdeen without any wound in your body.'

This strengthened the earl's resolve and he faced the queen's army only to be defeated at the Hill of Fare, to the north of Banchory. Huntly was captured unwounded but fell from his horse in an apoplexy. His body lay at the Tolbooth of Aberdeen, unmarked, to fulfil the witches' prophecy.

BIRNAM Perth and Kinross
Dunsinane, Birnam and Scone are all Perthshire locations associated with Macbeth, and local tradition points out the Witches' Stone of Macbeth at St Martins. At this anvil-shaped stone Macbeth is said to have consulted the witches who advised him to move his residence from Cairnbeddie to Dunsinane Hill and launch himself into immortality.

C

CARDEAN Tayside
Witches gathered at the Witch Knowe for covens.

CARLOPS Borders
At Witch's Leap they still point out the haunt of a witch who lived at the foot of Carlops Hill.

CLOSEBURN Nithsdale
A cairn is to be found here at Auchencairn called Witches' Wa's [walls].

CLOVA Angus
The incidence of rowan trees at Glen Clova is attributed to witch activity in the vicinity; anyone who valued their person and property in the area planted a rowan tree in the garden to keep witches away. The *Register of the Privy Council* records the trial and execution of Margaret Edison (or Adamson) in 1662 who was deemed to have blighted the lives of folk in Glen Clova; she was one of the witches to be locked into the Forfar Witch Branks (or Bridle).

COLINTON Edinburgh City
Witches' Walk is the passage between the garden of Robert Louis Stevenson's (1850–94) cottage and the kirkyard. Stevenson was interested in the 'bogey men' that surrounded Scottish witch lore and remembered the stories told to him of witchcraft by his nurse Alison Cunningham. He

mentions the testing of a witch by the water ordeal in *Thrawn Janet* (1881).

F

FAULDSHOPE Borders

Witch's Hill, at what was once called Falsehope, was named after the witch consulted by Michael Scott of Oakwood Tower. His story was woven into a Border witch tale that is typical of its genre. Here's a version collected by Winifred Petrie in the 1940s:

'While Michael Scott was living at Oakwood Tower, he heard about a certain witch who had a great reputation for her skill in magic, so he decided to pay her a visit to prove whether what people said about her was true.

'One day while out walking with his dogs he called on her, but although they talked a long time she pretended that she did not know any magic tricks, and would not show him anything. While they were speaking the warlock [Michael Scott] absentmindedly laid his stick on the table. In the twinkling of an eye the witch snatched it up and used it in such a way that he was turned into a hare.

Even his own hounds did not know him and gave chase. Away they ran over the fields and through hedges, the hare bounding in front for dear life. He succeeded in reaching Oakwood Tower before them, and hid in a drain till he had an opportunity of undoing the witch's spell.

'After that he waited his chance to have his revenge on her. Next year at harvest-time he again went that way with his dogs and some men. At a short distance from her house, just out of sight, they waited while one of his men was sent ahead to beg of the witch some bread for his dogs.

'Just as they expected, she refused to give him any bread and went in and shut the door. The man then did as Michael Scott had instructed him to do, if the witch should be rude; he fixed up a little placard over the door. On it the warlock had written these words, mixed up with several magical characters:

MAISTER MICHAEL SCOTT'S MAN SOCHT BREID AND GAT NANE

'The warlock's party then retired to a safe distance to watch what would happen.

'As soon as the words were fastened on her doorway the witch, who had been making porridge for the farm-workers, started to dance around the kitchen in circles, repeating the words on the door. Round and round she jigged, shrieking hilariously.

'Not long after the harvesters came back from the field for their dinner. No sooner had they passed under the magic writing than they also joined the witch's dance. The din from the house was ear-splitting, with laughing and shouting and stamping of feet.

'The farmer himself began to think something was the matter, and was on the point of going towards the farmhouse when he noticed Michael Scott and his men taking a keen interest in the affair from a distance. So instead of going straight into the house he went round cautiously and peeped in at the window.

'There was pandemonium. Half-dead with exhaustion, the witch was dragged round the house by the farm-workers, about the table and over the stools, all shouting the rhyme at the top of their voices.

'Fortunately for him the farmer did not pass under the doorway, but went right up to Michael Scott and asked for an explanation. Thinking that the witch had now had enough, the warlock told the farmer how to break the spell—by going backwards into the house and then taking down the writing with his left hand.

'This he did, and the dance stopped at once. But it was a lesson to the people in that district to be careful not to provoke the warlock again to anger.'

The story mentions magic writing and magic signs. Scotland's witch hunters supposed that witches had their own alphabet and a whole portfolio of secret signs, some of which are given opposite.

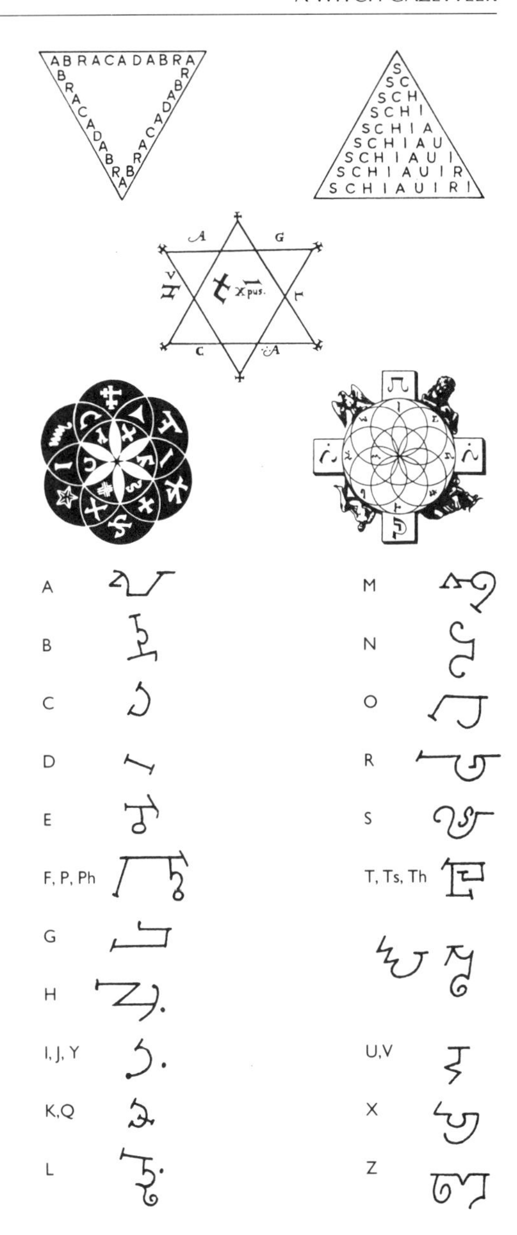
ABRACADABRA
S
SC
SCH
SCHI
SCHIA
SCHIAU
SCHIAUI
SCHIAUIR
SCHIAUIRI
A
G
L
A
C
Xpus.
A
B
C
D
E
F, P, Ph
G
H
I, J, Y
K,Q
L
M
N
O
R
S
T, Ts, Th
U,V
X
Z

FORFAR Angus

The museum at Forfar has in its collection the famous 'Witch Bridle'. This is an iron gag worn by 17th-century witches on their way to execution. During the Forfar witch trials of 1661, 1662 and 1666 the populace were afraid that witches would curse them as they were taken to the stake, so they locked them into the bridle to keep them quiet; the bridle inhibited talk by securing the tongue.

This instrument was known to have been used in the Forfar witch case of 1661 in which the witch most feared, Helen Guthrie, was forced to wear it.

It was long the custom in Scotland for parishes to own a similar gag known as a Branks; this was used by magistrates to stop women berating their husbands after they had been found guilty of being a scold.

FORRES Moray

Duncan I (1034–40) held his court at Forres and it was on their way there that Macbeth and Banquo were reputed to have met, on the 'blasted heath', the 'weird sisters', the three witches for whom Forres was notorious. At Forres is the Witches' Stone marking the spot of the executions of Isobel Elder and Isabel Simson in 1663.

G

GASK Perth and Kinross

At the Witch Knowe witches were executed.

GORDONSTOUN Moray

Now the seat of one of the world's most prominent public schools, Gordonstoun was acquired from the Gordon-Cummings of Altyre. Once, though, it was the home of one of Scotland's most infamous aristocratic witches, Sir Robert Gordon (1647–1704).

In 1678 local stories tell how Sir Robert avoided death by giving his shadow to the Devil. In Scotland's north-east it was believed that a person's shadow was the manifestation of his soul, and everyone knew that because of their evil working witches cast no shadow. To avoid having to give the Devil any further gifts Sir Robert built for himself a Devil-proof fortress at Gordonstoun known as the Round Square, and there he planted himself with a minister for company.

The minister persuaded Sir Robert that he could never be any safter than in a church and the pair made their way to Birnie church a few miles south of Elgin, but on the way the Devil waylaid Sir Robert. The locals explained Sir Robert's death in 1704 as this encounter with the Devil, who they said slung the knight over his shoulder and galloped with him to the 'Fires of Hell', with 'a huge demon dog running beside them with its fangs buried deep' in Sir Robert's neck.

I

INNERWICK East Lothian
The Witch's Cairn is to be found on Crystal Rig. From her the local witches worked magic to bewitch boats in the Firth of Forth and the North Sea.

INNERLEITHEN Tweeddale
The Witches' Dancing Ground is at Mirchmoor Hill; there is a site of the same name at the Border village of Traquair at Salter-Sykes.

J

JEDBURGH Roxburgh
At the Goose Pool, Townfoot Brig, witches were subject to the ordeal of ducking. The town had serious witch mania in 1586–87, 1613, 1628 and 1671. The *Register of the Privy Council* for 1586 notes with great disdain that the witch Helene Elliot deliberately absented herself from the court 'in high contempt of our Sovereign Lord and his authority'.

K

KEMNAY Gordon
This Aberdeenshire site of the Lang Stane O'Craigearn contains a standing stone around which witches convened.

L

LAMBERTON Berwickshire
The Witches' Knowe lies west of the ruined church of Lamberton at Mordington Hill. This was an execution site for witches around 1700.

LUNAN Angus
A place made famous for its witch ducking pool.

M

MARYKIRK Kincardine and Deeside
The Witch Hillock here, probably an ancient burial barrow, was long pointed out as a meeting place for witch sabbats.

MENMUIR Angus
Local legend has it that the hillfort known as White Caterthun was a stronghold built by local witches as a base for the fairyfolk. A witch, the story went, carried the stones for the fort's ramparts in her apron. Along with the Brown Caterthun hillfort the site was inspiration for Sir Walter Scott's verses of 1796:

> Or if we trust the village tale
> A wayward maid in witching hour
> When stars were red and moon was pale
> Reared thy dread mound by magic power.

MUSSELBURGH East Lothian
Witches were burned at the Bogie Hole, once visited during the traditional Riding of the Marches. The town had famous witch trials in 1603, 1609, 1628 and 1661. During the trial of Bessie Fouler in the latter year, local records say, the Devil was so angry at her prosecution that he raised a great storm to prevent the execution.

N

NEWTON-STEWART Wigtownshire
Witches gathered for sabbats at Locharbrigknowe.

NORTH BALLACHULISH Lochaber
The Split Stone, located on the north side of Loch Leven, is linked in local legend with the story of the Witch Gormul. It was in the days of Sir Ewen Cameron of Lochiel (1629–1719) and the famous Highlander was accosted one morning by a *cailleach* (hag), the Witch Gormul. To escape her attentions Sir Ewen leapt into a boat and rowed away. As he pulled from the shore she shouted after him: 'Blessings on you Ewen', her way of disguising a curse. Still rowing, Sir Ewen replied 'Your blessings be on yonder grey stone, hag', whereupon the stone split in two.

The story may owe much to the race memory of a tribal goddess, for some time ago a wooden figure of a *cailleach* was found buried in the peat near to the site of the old Ballachulish ferry-landing along with a wickerwork shrine. The eyes of the figure were inlaid with quartz pebbles, a stone of reputed magic powers in the Highlands.

O

OLDHAMSTOCKS East Lothian
The Witches' Cairn is the site of supposed witch sabbats.

THE OCHILS
The range of hills known as the Ochils runs for 24 miles, taking in parts of the old Scottish counties of Clackmannan, Kinross and Fife and a large part of south-east Perthshire. Its streams, pools, tracks and forest land have long been mentioned as locations for witch covens. Many place names reflect this, for example Carlin's Craig, Warlock Glen, Devil's Loch and Deil's Bucket in the region most associated with witches above Logie and Blairlogie. Writing of this area in 1851 Charles Roger mentions how there were many 'ill-favoured old women' who were remembered for their supposed witchcraft skills. The most celebrated witchcraft case at Logie was the trial of Bessie Finlaysoune on 16 July 1618. In 1658 Black Kate of Parsons-Leys and Auld Meg of Ashintrool were

accused of witchcraft-inspired murders at Grange, Tullibody and Clackmannan.

At Crook of Devon in 1662 a whole coven was arrested and eleven of its members were executed immediately after the trial; the twelfth seems to have escaped 'justice' for a while.

Ochils witchlore has left a legacy of verses too in local history. Lochy Faulds at the foot of Gloom Hill supplies one example:

> In Quarry Burn, the witches meet,
> Syne through the air, they scour fu' fleet,
> They flee, and they flee.
> Till they reach Lochy Faulds
> Whaur Auld Nick in person
> His tribunal holds.

P

PETTERDEN Tayside
Tradition has it that witch gatherings took place here at the Loch of Forfar.

R

RATHO Lothian
An ancient cup-marked stone near Tormain Hill has long had the name 'The Witches' Stone'.

S

SAINT ANDREWS Fife
Set at the west end of the Scores is the famed 'Witch Pool' where suspects were subjected to the water ordeal. Witch trials were held in St Andrews at frequent intervals between 1569 and 1667. They even included cases tried before the Civil Court. One such example comes from 1569; recorded in *Historie and life of King James the Sext,* it tells how Sir William Stewart, Lyon King of Arms, was hanged 'for divers points of witchcraft and necromancy'.

SAMUELSTON East Lothian
Famous for the purges of Earls of Haddington against witches, who were 'rooted out' in 1612, 1661—a bumper year of four witch trials—and

1662. The Rev John Bull of nearby Gladsmuir used the cases as the basis of his manual on how to recognize a witch.

SCALLOWAY Shetland
Walk across the Gallows Hill, some two miles out of Scalloway, and you will see the ashes of the many witch burnings still visible in the soil. Shetland's contribution to witch mania lasted from 1603 to around 1700, the last case being the execution of Barbara Tulloch and Ellen King on Law Tingholm, Tingwall Loch.

SMOO CAVES Sutherland
Smoo Caves, Durness, are connected with tales of the Devil. Here, tradition has it, the first Lord Reay, known as Donald, the Wizard of Reay, had a famous encounter with Satan. It seems that during a grand tour of Italy, Reay first met the Devil who encouraged him to study the Black Arts. In the 17th century it was fashionable for the aristocracy to study the supernatural and Reay proved to be a ready pupil. Superstition had it that at the end of such studies the Devil would select a disciple. Reay was chosen and the Devil marked him by removing his shadow.

One night, Donald Reay was exploring the greatest Smoo Cave with his dog when he disturbed his former mentor and three witches practising magic. Trapped by Donald Reay and his dog the Devil blew holes in the cave roof and the sinister quartet flew away. This was the explanation for the holes through which the Smoo Burn flows today.

Incidentally, in the Aberdeenshire parish of Skene they used to tell a similar story about Alexander Skene, bynamed the 'Wizard Laird of Skene'.

SOUTH KNAPDALE Strathclyde
The Argyllshire Carse Standing Stones were traditionally the location for a battle between two clans. One side was apparently aided by a witch who, strange to tell, could only work spells when

on horseback. The enemy side pushed her off her horse and won the battle.

SOUTH UIST Outer Hebrides
Leac na bana bhuidreach, the 'Witch's Gravestone', is a chambered cairn long credited as a magic place.

SPOTT East Lothian
The Witches' Stone is where Marion Lillie, bynamed the 'Rigwoodie Witch', was executed in 1698 and where 'many witches' were burned up to 1705. 'Rigwoodie' means stubborn, or bony, and given to pranks. Several witches were indicted at Spott in 1624 and 1661.

SWONA Orkney
A Ronaldsay witch, whose name none can recall, once loved a local man. In a fit of pique when the man went off with another woman, she bewitched the woman and made her jump from a boat in which she was sailing with her sweetheart. The man dived in to save her and both were soon in difficulties. Repenting, the witch grabbed the man's hand to pull him and his companion to safety but all were lost. The Wells of Swona is a whirlpool said to have been formed out of the witch's struggles to save them.

T

TORRIDON Ross and Cromarty
Here people used wood from the bird-cherry to make walking-sticks and tethering-posts and in house construction to keep witches away. The witches of Torridon were skilled in staunching blood from poisoned wounds with this recitation:

> Be your poison within the ground
> May your pain be within the hill.
> Wholeness be to the wound
> Rest be to the hurt.

TORRYBURN Fife
The Rev Allan Logan had the reputation of being

one of Scotland's most zealous witch hunters. He held the ministry at Torryburn during 1695–1717 and the *Kirk Session Minutes* show that he did not shirk his self-appointed duty as witch harrier. Torryburn had conducted witch examinations in 1630 and 1666, but Logan was to make the 1704 case notorious in Scotland's witch history.

In June 1704 one Jean Bissett reported that she had been 'molested by Satan' through the ministrations of 'some particular persons' bearing the 'Devil's mark'. She cited 72-year-old Lilias Adie, Janet Whyte and Mary Neilson as her persecutors. Ecstatic that he could now enhance his reputation as a witch hunter the Rev Logan set about collecting evidence against the women. Of Whyte and Neilson he could find nothing incriminating and they appear to have been absolved. Logan now concentrated his attentions on the clearly senile, even deranged, Lilias Adie. In no time he had her admitting 'that the Devil bade her attend many meetings' and making such statements as 'I am in compact with the Devil'. Lilias Adie was arrested and put in the local lockup; to the Rev Logan's disappointment she died there. His last act was to deny her Christian burial, and she was interred 'within the floodmark between Torryburn and Torrie'. And there she rested until 1875 when she was disinterred and her skull acquired by the local antiquary Joseph Neil Paton, who bequeathed it to the University of St Andrews. No further witch investigations took place at Torryburn after the Rev Logan left.

U

URQUHART Moray
Here is located a stone circle known as the Nine Deils' Stanes; walk round these three times at midnight, the old folk averred, and you would see the Devil appear.

V

VALLAY Outer Hebrides
The Witch's Pit can never be filled in, according to local superstition. Once a witch was thrown into

this pit for stealing milk while in the form of a hare, and now as material is put into the pit the witch ejects it in an attempt to scramble out.

W

WATERSIDE HILL Galloway

The 'Witches' Score' (from the Scots to mark or to scratch) is an elliptical area defined by a depression in the surrounding soil. Tradition has it that a farmer, Andrew Forrester of Knocksheen, was assailed nearby by witches one night in 1750 or thereabouts as he was making his way home from an inn at St John's Clachan of Dalry.

As he passed the ruined kirk at Motte of Dalry he saw its old stones lit up and a coven taking place with frenetic dancing led by the fiddler Davie McClemmet. Forrester reined in his horse and in his enthusiasm he shouted out; the witches thus disturbed at their illegal gathering gave chase and Forrester feared for his life. Remembering an anti-witch ritual, he dismounted and with the tip of his swordblade scratched out an oval shape around him in the grass and said the words of incantation: 'I draw this score in the name of God Almighty and may nae evil ever pass over it.'

Unable to cross the score, the witches attempted to lure Forrester's horse out of the marked area. They failed, but one of them—maybe the Devil himself some said—grabbed the horse's tail and pulled it out. As dawn rose the witches fled and Forrester went home.

Soon he returned to the spot and with a spade dug out a more permanent refuge; thereafter generations of his family (and subsequent owners of his farm) kept the outline fresh.

Y

YARROW Ettrick and Lauderdale

Around the time that James Graham, 5th Earl and 1st Marquis of Montrose (1612–50) defeated the Covenanters at the nearby Battle of Philiphaugh in 1645, a witch tale was circulating in Yarrow. A young blacksmith's apprentice was regularly tormented by a witch, who would enter his bedroom each night and place a magic bridle over his head. Instantly the boy was transformed into a horse, and the witch galloped off astride him to her coven.

Learning of this, the apprentice's older brother changed places with him one night. The witch tethered the young man (in his transformation as a horse) to a tree while she went to her coven. With a toss of his head the horse slipped the magic bridle off, and instantly turned back into the young man. He waited for the witch to return; when she did he managed to slip the bridle over her head and galloped her back to the forge. There he shod the witch-horse, and next day the witch was found in her garden writhing in agony with horseshoes nailed to her feet and hands.